The Perfect Christmas

ANTHEA TURNER

Virgin BOOKS

To my mum, who struggled through many Christmases with no help from me – sorry.

Published by Virgin Books 2008

2 4 6 8 10 9 7 5 3

First published in Great Britain in 2008 by
Virgin Books
Random House, 20 Vauxhall Bridge Road,
London SW1V 2SA

www.virginbooks.com
www.rbooks.co.uk

Addresses for companies within The Random House Group Limited can be found at:
www.randomhouse.co.uk/offices.htm

The Random House Group Limited Reg. No. 954009

A CIP catalogue record for this book is available from the British Library

ISBN 9781905264414

The Random House Group Limited supports The Forest Stewardship Council [FSC], the leading international forest certification organisation. All our titles that are printed on Greenpeace approved FSC certified paper carry the FSC logo. Our paper procurement policy can be found at www.rbooks.co.uk/environment

Mixed Sources
Product group from well-managed forests and other controlled sources
www.fsc.org Cert no. TT-COC-2139
© 1996 Forest Stewardship Council

Printed and bound by Firmengruppe APPL, aprinta druck, Wemding, Germany

Contents

Introduction

'I hate Christmas – to me it's just a load of work and hassle on top of everything else I do around this house. And furthermore, no one else lifts a finger. You just sit back and think the fairies do everything. Well, let me tell you, next year I'm not doing anything and you can sort it out yourselves!'

This complaint is often shouted by a woman somewhere around the second week of December when Christmas is sounding like anything but a celebration.

Thankfully for the survival of the festive season, the women of the nation seem to have selective amnesia and somewhere around the middle of November start gearing up for another battle which will probably end like all the others that have gone before.

So let's here and now agree to change: instead of leaving it until the last minute in the vain hope that Christmas will be cancelled, let's resolve to be prepared and organised so that we too can enjoy what for everyone else is a joyous occasion.

Imagine yourself now, with the hindsight of maturity, doing an exam. You wouldn't leave it until the night before as some of us did when we were at school. No, sense tells us that if we tackle revising little and often, come the big day there's no stress or panic and we sail through with flying colours.

Please, please don't spend ridiculous amounts of money – be creative and clever with your buying. Remember, it's only one day of the year. Christmas lunch is just a roast with a cracker and God never meant for you to get your knickers in a twist over His son's birthday, which probably wasn't even on 25 December.

This book gives you lots of choices so that you can create a Christmas which is tailored to the time you have available, your budget and the needs of you and your family. But whatever choices you make there is one strong and underlying message: START EARLY. And however mad or pedantic you think I am on that one, believe me it works. You will spend less money, be more relaxed and, dare I say it, even have a smug smile on your face when your friends are running round like headless chickens, or should I say turkeys!

Use all the handy tips and advice in this book to make this year your best and most perfect Christmas ever.

Frances Turner x

1

The Perfect
Christmas

We all want Christmas to be perfect – carols, crackling log fires, twinkling trees, stunning decorations and fabulous food. Unfortunately, it doesn't just happen. Christmas is hard work, but it can be fun if you get organised and don't leave everything to the last minute.

If we're honest, there seem to be two ways of doing Christmas:

- **Option 1:** An exhausting – and expensive – three-week whirlwind of shopping, cooking and decorating

- **Option 2:** An organised countdown with no Christmas Eve shopping expeditions, late-night trips to the garage for flowers or the off-licence for a few more bottles of wine

Take the first option and all you'll want to do is collapse in an armchair on Christmas Day, bury your head under a cushion and forget about the looming bills. Take the second option and you'll sail through, calm, contented and as sparkling as your celebrations.

It seems obvious. So why do so many of us take the first option, even though we vow each New Year to get organised in time for NEXT Christmas? *The Perfect Christmas* will help you to make panic a thing of the past.

If you aren't a domestic goddess for the other fifty-one weeks of the year, don't try to be one at Christmas. No one will think any less of you if you cheat a little and buy some pre-prepared food. And with a few simple tricks they won't even notice! If you do want to do all the cooking yourself, you can lessen the load by cooking and freezing dishes weeks ahead.

Get your present buying and wrapping out of the way early, order as much as you can and have it delivered to dodge the crowds, and make lists, lists and more lists so nothing is forgotten.

Remember delegation – there is no law that says you have to do Christmas all by yourself. Use a little psychology when you're sharing out the tasks. Write down everything that you'd like someone to do and ask the family to choose tasks for themselves. If they get a choice they are more likely to help willingly. It'll be easier then for you to assign any jobs that are left over.

Make *The Perfect Christmas* your ultimate festive companion. It's not intended as a blueprint for you to follow to the letter, but simply a handy source of inspiration, short cuts, ideas and solutions to dip into year after year. You'll all have your own special traditions and customs that you'll want to weave into your celebrations, meals that make Christmas special for your family and treasured decorations that you like to get out each year. That's as it should be, but you'll also find scores of ideas to add to your festivities.

Whether this is the first Christmas feast you have prepared or the twentieth, you'll discover fresh inspiration in the pages of this book.

Totally practical and beautifully illustrated, this book will help you decide what to buy and what to make yourself, how to make your festive entertaining memorable and how to add a touch of style and glamour to the celebrations. You'll discover how to save time and money, and what you can make if you have time to spare.

Whatever your budget there are hints and ideas to help you decorate your home and Christmas tree, personalise your presents and create special meals. There are also quizzes, games to play and suggestions for fun days out with family and friends.

The early bird . . .

It's never too early to get the show on the road, but you don't have to go at it like Mother Christmas on a mission as soon as January arrives. Just keep your eyes open for perfect presents, things you know you'll need or plan to replace, then buy them and store them away. Shop wisely and you'll save pounds.

Almost as soon as we come back from our summer holidays, shelves in the shops are groaning under the weight of every kind of Christmas item imaginable. Don't close your eyes, put your head down and walk by. Take the opportunity to pick up non-perishable items that you know you will need. It'll help spread the financial load as well as easing the stress in the hectic weeks up to Christmas when you're trying to juggle work, home life and a hundred and one other tasks. By getting organised you'll have time to actually enjoy the preparations, perhaps make some edible gifts, some very special decorations for your home, and get your freezer full of festive food.

2

Countdown to Christmas

The Eight-week Plan

Make your own countdown calendar – it will help to keep you on track. And starting your preparations early means you will have less, not more, to do as the big day approaches.

Eight weeks before

- Plan your Christmas meals – make lists of all the food and drink you will need.

- Plan your Christmas entertaining – make lists of everything you'll need.

- Send out your invitations.

- Place orders for drinks and food. Remember to order your Christmas meat.

- Check you've got enough cutlery, china and glasses, particularly if you're entertaining. If you're short of large serving dishes and bowls try to borrow from a friend before going out and buying or hiring them. Order any glasses, china or equipment you will need to hire, or try Homebase and Ikea, which can sometimes be cheaper than hiring.

- Write out your gift list. Set a budget and try to stick to it.

- If you are making your own Christmas cards, start now – if you haven't already made them.

- Plan the theme for your Christmas decorations.

- Buy Christmas wrapping paper, ribbons and trimmings if you didn't stock up in the January sales.

- Start adding a few Christmas items to your weekly shop.

- If you are making them, now is the time to make your Christmas cake and pudding.

- Check last posting dates and write them on your calendar. Don't forget overseas dates, if you need them.

- Book Christmas and New Year taxis.

- Arrange a baby-sitter if you are going to need one at any time in December. They'll quickly get booked up, especially over weekends.

- Clean out the freezer – it's time to dump the mystery packages lurking in the depths. Try to use up as much food as you can to make room for your Christmas foods.

- Have a pre-Christmas turn-out in the house.

Six weeks before

- Start buying your gifts – and wrapping them to save time later.

- Place any online orders for gifts to make the most of regular posting rates.

- Plan the theme for your dining table and buy any accessories, such as crackers.

- Check your table linen.

Four weeks before

- Start cooking dishes for the freezer – meals for the family, plus dishes for entertaining.

- If you are making mince pies, do them now and pop them into the freezer.

- Buy your Christmas cake and pudding if you are not making them.

- Get your Christmas cards written and ready to post. If you can, put the addresses on the computer and print them out on adhesive labels. Save the file and you won't have to do it again next year.

- If you're planning to do a supermarket shop online book a delivery slot – deliveries for the week before Christmas are quickly booked up.

- Do any last-minute online present shopping so there is still time to get to the shops if the gift you want is out of stock.

Three weeks before

- Post your UK Christmas parcels and cards.

- Cook and freeze sauces, desserts and vegetable dishes that can be made ahead.

- Make/buy and freeze a few 'family suppers' for the busy days before Christmas.

- Locate the nutcrackers and corkscrews – two vital gadgets that have a habit of disappearing.

- Finish your gift shopping.

- Prepare your guest room.

Two weeks before

- Post any last-minute cards or parcels.

- Buy your tree, but bring it into the house as late as possible.

- Decorate your front door with a wreath.

- Ice and decorate the Christmas cake, if you've made one.

- Buy or collect evergreens and other foliage for Christmas decorations and arrangements.

- Order non-perishable foods and have them delivered.

- Order flowers to be delivered next week.

Tips for a stress-free Christmas

1. Don't try to do everything alone. Accept every offer of help you can get.

2. Be realistic with your entertaining. Keep gatherings small and informal.

3. Don't let Christmas spending spiral out of control.

4. Check your 'to do list'. Cross off everything that isn't essential and underline every task you can delegate and delegate NOW.

One week before

- Decorate the house and Christmas tree.

- Shop for any foods that you need to see or touch before buying. Leave buying fresh food as late as you can.

- If you've got a frozen turkey check how long it will take to defrost. Make a note on the calendar, so you don't forget to take it out of the freezer in time.

Christmas Eve

- Lay the table.
- Prepare as much as you can for the Christmas meal.
- Get out all the serving dishes you will need.
- Prepare the after-dinner coffee tray.

Finally, hang up the stockings, put the champagne on ice, relax and get ready to enjoy the celebrations.

If you're short of time

Here are some simple time-savers:

- Lots of shops sell stamps, so beat the queues in the Post Office by buying them at a shop you're already visiting.

- You'll get the shopping done in half the time if you don't have the children in tow, so ask a friend to mind them for an hour or two. Do the same for her.

- Buy inexpensive gift bags and boxes, some packets of tissue, and some ribbon, bows and trimmings. Wrap a gift in tissue, pop it in the box or bag, add a pretty trimming and the job's done. It's so much quicker than measuring and cutting wrapping paper.

- It may not be imaginative but gift vouchers are a speedy solution to those 'whatever can I buy them?' dilemmas. It'll save hours walking round the shops looking for inspiration. You can always combine the gift voucher with an associated gift. If you buy a garden voucher add a couple of packets of seeds. Many large stores sell vouchers and gift cards online.

- If you're not set on giving a 'surprise' gift, ask the person you're buying the present for for some ideas. It'll save you time and you'll know you're buying a gift they'd like.

- If you're looking for a specific gift, phone around the shops before you leave home to see if they have it in stock. See if they will reserve it for you.

The Christmas clean

Before things get really hectic, set aside some time to get the house clean and tidy. Make sure you get the rest of the family involved.

- Tackle the house room by room – you don't have to do it all at once.

- Tidy away clutter, throw away everything you no longer need, or bag it up to take to the charity shop.

- Don't miss the 'cleaning blind spots' – the cobwebs in the lampshades, empty shampoo bottles in the bathroom, finger marks on the lamp switches, and dusty bookshelves.

With the Christmas clean out of the way it's plain sailing.

Safety first

- Make a list of emergency numbers and stick them in a handy place – inside the door of one of the kitchen cupboards is a good idea. Make sure everyone knows where it is.

- Check smoke alarms.

- Check your first-aid kit and stocks of painkillers, indigestion remedies etc.

- Make sure the family have supplies of any prescribed medications to last over Christmas and the New Year when surgeries and pharmacies may be closed.

- Check you have batteries for torches, and that everyone knows where they are kept.

- Turn off Christmas-tree lights and fairy lights before you go out and when you go to bed.

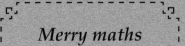

Merry maths

Mathematicians have calculated that Santa would need 200,000 reindeer flying at 200,000 times the speed of light to be able to deliver presents to every child in the world on Christmas night. No one seems to have calculated how much the presents would weigh!

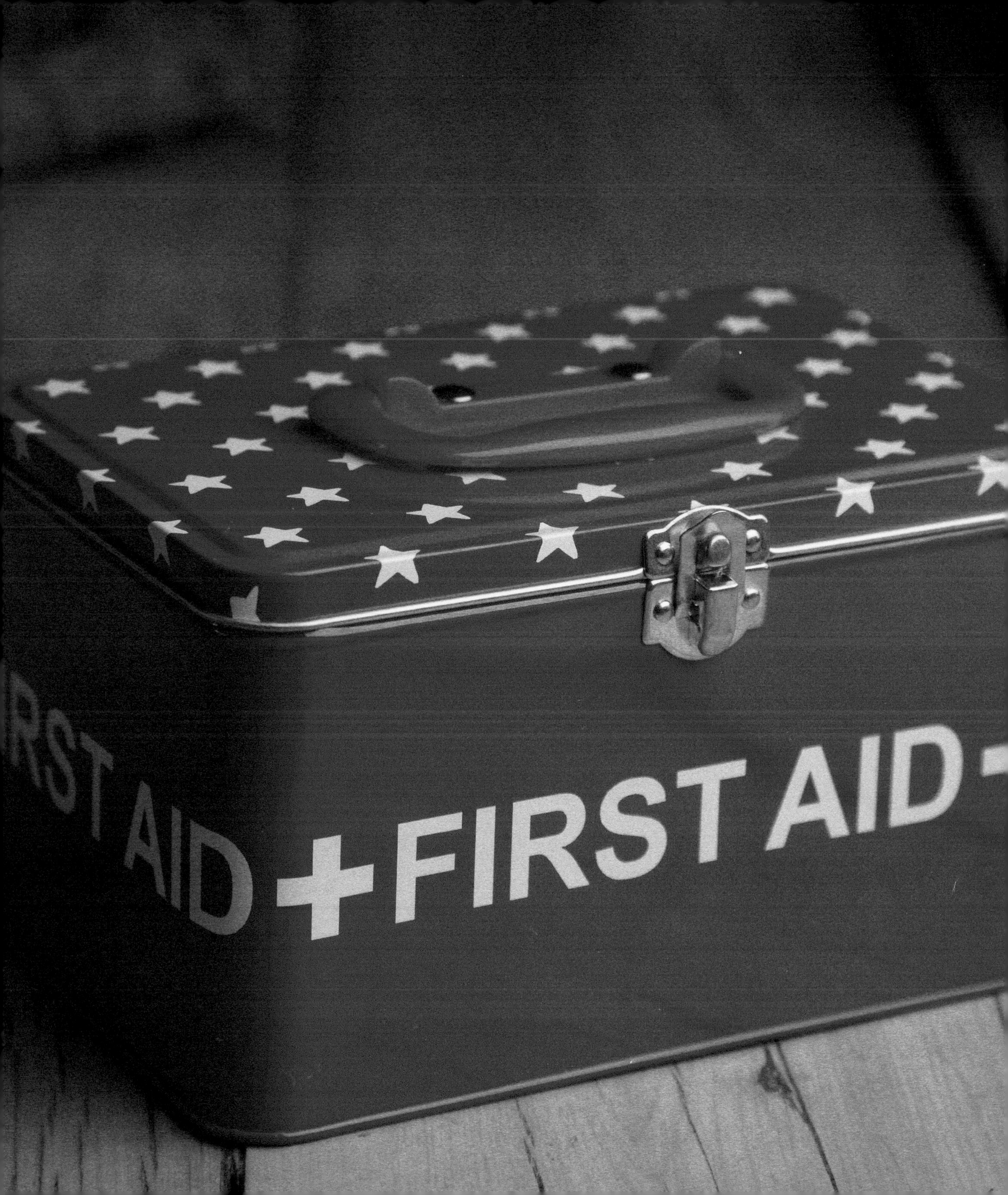

RST AID
FIRST AID

CHAMPNEYS
SPA SKIN CARE

Chamomile & Ro...
Moistur...
Miracle Mas...

Hydrates, sooth...
revitalises super...

CHAMPNEYS
NATURALS

Citrus Glow
Energising
Shower Gel

Invigorates, revitalises
and cleanses your skin

Michael Bublé
& Frank Sinatra

CHAMPNEYS

MPN
Exotic Body

3

Gifts Galore

Gift Ideas

You don't have to have pots of money to find the perfect gift. Be imaginative, and have fun choosing something special. Think about the hobbies and special interests of the person you are buying the gift for. Could you find something associated with one of them? Or what about a collection of small themed gifts?

If you're short of inspiration, try the Internet for ideas. It's also a good place to go shopping if you are short of time and know what you want to buy. An hour spent ordering gifts online (or ordering a load of grocery shopping) will save you three hours looking for somewhere to park, trailing around the shops, and queuing to pay.

Get started on your shopping as soon as you can. You'll find more choice, and avoid the crowds. Always remember to take your shopping lists with you!

Gift collections

Collections of small gifts are great fun to put together and to receive.

For a footy-mad youngster

Make or buy a large gift bag, containing a glass jar with sweets in the team's colours, a football scarf or maybe a ticket to a match. Pin a team rosette on the bag.

For the nature lover

Buy a birdseed feeder and a peanut feeder, along with seeds and nuts, and perhaps a coconut shell filled with fat and seeds. Or consider buying a bird table, a bird box, a ladybird box or a bee box.

For a keen gardener

Buy a watering can or wooden trug, and fill it with a pair of gardening gloves, seeds, plant labels and a skein of raffia. Cover the trug with cellophane and attach a large cellophane bow. (If you can't buy cellophane to make a bow, buy one from your local florist.)

Or for a lady gardener buy a gardening apron and fill the pockets with string, packets of her favourite seeds, plant labels and a pair of pretty but practical gardening gloves and some hand cream.

A pampering box

Buy a basket and fill it with a favourite magazine, some scented candles and a selection of bath-time goodies.

For a plant lover

Buy an olive tree and an attractive ceramic waterproof container. Tie a large loose-weave ribbon bow around the pot and attach a label to the trunk of the tree. Or attach a few tiny bows or bunches of feathers to the plant to give it a festive look.

For the student

Buy a jute shopping bag and fill it with the essentials of student life – a couple of mugs, a large jar of coffee, an iTunes card, a subscription to a magazine they like, cinema vouchers . Or give them a supermarket shopping token or card – it'll help their money go further.

A mulled wine kit

Buy a ridged cardboard box and a bottle of red wine, an attractive glass storage jar filled with muslin bags of mulled wine spices and a box of homemade biscuits.

For the foodie

Baskets filled with luxury or ethnic foods always make special presents for foodies. You could put together baskets of:

- Flavoured oils and vinegars, olives, bottled pimentos, garlic, breadsticks

- Curry spices, Indian chutney, basmati rice, poppadums

- Oriental spices, soy sauce, sesame oil, jasmine rice

- Savoury biscuits, cheese, chutney and a half-bottle of port

- A special tea, a small fruitcake and some luxury biscuits

If you want to save money

These ideas will help keep the cash in your pocket.

- Take advantage of 'early bird' special offers on Christmas food and drink. Start looking for them in early November – or even earlier.

- Entertaining? Invite friends over to tea or for brunch, rather than throwing an evening party – you'll save loads on drink.

- If you are buying gifts for a couple, buy a joint present they can both enjoy.

- Look out for two-for-one and three-for-two offers on gifts.

- Making your own hampers of Christmas goodies could save pounds – it also means that you choose what goes into them.

- Delay buying Christmas food until you have made your lists. There is an awful lot of temptation on the supermarket shelves and you could easily end up with a cupboard full of things you don't use.

- If you enjoy cooking and have time, spend a day in the kitchen making edible gifts – they are always appreciated.

- Use a price-comparison website to find the best price if you are buying a large item. Try www.kelkoo.co.uk or www.pricerunner.co.uk.

Shopping on the Internet

Shopping online can be a real time-saver. Start ordering as early as you can as popular lines may sell out. Also check on delivery dates and if it's an important item allow enough time to get an alternative from a shop if it does not arrive in time. If you are out at work all day it is a good idea to check whether the company is prepared to deliver your parcel to a neighbour.

Tips

- Give yourself time to check a few websites before ordering so you can compare prices and any special offers.

- Order early to take advantage of standard delivery charges rather than having to pay extra for express services.

- Always print out a copy of your order or confirmation of your order, in case you need to chase it up. Make a note of the telephone number if it doesn't appear on the order form.

- Avoid ordering from websites which do not show a postal address and telephone number.

- Check there is a padlock symbol in one of the corners of the screen before entering your credit card details.

- NEVER reveal your PIN number over the Internet or any password associated with the card you are using.

- If you are ordering from a company for the first time then check out the customer reviews on websites such as www.reviewcentre.co.uk and www.ciao.co.uk.

Anthea's Top Tip

Doing at least some of your grocery shopping online makes sense. If it's boring or bulky like kitchen towels, toilet rolls, pet food, baby supplies, tins, soft drinks and isn't something that you need to see or touch – order it, and have it delivered. You can spend the time saved doing something more interesting.

Christmas cards

Buying, making, or sending an Internet card – the choice is yours. Hand-made cards are very special and becoming very popular. But if you've got an extensive Christmas card list, it can be time-consuming.

Buying cards

There is a fantastic range in the shops and on websites. Buy early to get the widest choice. It's also a great opportunity to support your favourite charities.

Making cards

The options are endless. If you are short of ideas, check out the Christmas issues of magazines or look in the library for books on card-making. Here are some ideas:

- Buy a pre-made rubber stamp with a Christmas image from stationers and hobby shops or create your own using a paper stencil or potato stencil. Use different kinds and colours of ink to stamp designs on to pre-folded cards. (Keep potato stencils in water until you are ready to use them so they do not discolour. When you are ready to make your cards dry the potato thoroughly on kitchen towel before applying the paint or ink.)

- As an alternative you could have a stamp made from a child's drawing and use this to print your own cards. You'll find companies who make inexpensive stamps on the Internet. You can also use your stamp to decorate wrapping paper, bags and tags.

- To save time buy 'Christmas card kits' (the ones that contain all you need to decorate the card along with instructions, folded plain cards and envelopes) from a craft or hobby shop.

- Or design your own card and buy the individual elements you need from a craft shop.

E-cards

If you are short of time why not send e-cards to friends and family who have computers (perhaps sending the money saved to a charity). There are many websites – including charities – offering both free and paid-for e-cards. You can find everything from traditional cards to 'all singing, all dancing' animated versions. Or if you are good on the computer produce your own personalised image and attach it to an email.

Making your own family cards

Use your computer to help you create original and very personal family cards. Digital photographs of the family (perhaps a photo taken the previous Christmas), wintry scenes or scanned images of a child's painting can easily be printed on to a card, or printed on photo-quality paper and glued on to a bought ready-folded card.

Inexpensive packs of plain, ready-folded cards and envelopes can be found at stationers and craft shops.

If you haven't got a scanner and printer at home, try your library or take your images to a print shop where the staff will scan your images for you.

Displaying Christmas Cards

Stuck for a way to display your Christmas cards? Try one of these ideas.

- Fix three pieces of ribbon to the back of a door with a bow at the top of each and peg the cards to the ribbon.

- Make a decorative feature of cards in the hall by draping a piece of ribbon along the picture rail. Punch a hole in each of the cards and thread a short piece of ribbon through. Tie the cards along the draped ribbon at intervals.

- Buy one of the many card-holders that you can find in gift and card shops.

Anthea's Top Tip

Be careful when printing cards on the computer to work out the dimensions of your image in relation to the dimensions of the cards you are making. Think in advance about which side of the fold the image is going, whether it is portrait or landscape, and make sure that it is the right way up. You should be able to get two images on an A4 sheet. Alternatively you could print four images, cut them out and stick on to ready-folded cards.

4

Deck the Halls

Trends may swing from traditional gold and silver opulence, the rustic feel of natural materials, modern glitz or icy chic, but when it comes to decorating your home, it's your choice.

With a bit of imagination you can transform your house into a magical Christmas wonderland without burning the midnight oil or digging deep into your pockets.

You don't have to decorate every shelf and corner or festoon your rooms with garlands and tinsel. A welcoming Christmas wreath on the door, a beautifully decorated tree, a few festive arrangements or large sturdy vases of evergreens are all that is needed to create an elegant setting for your celebrations.

So, however you choose to 'deck your halls' here are some ideas and tips to help and inspire you.

Looking for inspiration?

If you are looking for decorating ideas that you can adapt for your own home and have some time to spare, visit:

- A Christmas craft fair

- An outdoor Christmas market – preferably in the late afternoon or evening when all the stalls are lit up, and warming mulled wine, mince pies and roasted chestnuts are being served

And don't forget to take a look at the Christmas window displays in the big stores and the November and December issues of magazines.

Festive Wreaths

A welcoming festive wreath on your front door sets the scene for your decorations.

If you're short of time and cash

Buy a basic conifer wreath and decorate it yourself, rather than starting from scratch, Here are some ways to transform a plain conifer wreath made of fir or pine branches into an eye-catching wreath.

A traditional wreath

Use florists' wire (you'll find it at florists and large garden centres) to fix some sprigs of ivy (sprayed gold or silver if you like) and waxy evergreen leaves from the garden to the basic wreath. Make some small bows of ribbon and wire these to the wreath. Finish off by wiring in some red or orange berries and some small pine cones. Add a large red bow at the top of the wreath and a loop of ribbon to hang the wreath to the door.

A natural wreath

Wire in some ivy leaves, rosemary sprigs and waxy evergreen leaves. Add bunches of cinnamon sticks tied with raffia, bunches of berries, bunches of small red chillies and fir cones. Tie a large bow at the top or bottom.

An ice-cool wreath

Give your wreath an ice-cool and modern look by adding waxy evergreen leaves (such as bay, laurel or box), sprigs of rosemary and some silvery eucalyptus twigs. Then maybe wire in some silver baubles, silver bells and bunches of white feathers. Finish by adding a large glittery white ribbon to the top of the wreath.

A winter fruits wreath

Add sprays of evergreen foliage such as rosemary, bay, holly or ivy to a conifer wreath. Then wire on clementines studded with cloves or slices of dried orange, small apples or bunches of bright orange berries. Finish with a large bow of ribbon.

If you're short of cash

Make a festive bough

Instead of a wreath, why not make a festive bough for your door? They look stunning and will only take a few minutes to make.

All you'll need is a bunch of mixed evergreen foliage – preferably with some berries – and some ribbon. (See if you can scavenge foliage from your garden or from friends. If you can't you'll find inexpensive bunches of evergreens in supermarkets, garden centres and florists in the weeks leading up to Christmas.)

Wind a piece of string around the neck of the bunch and tie tightly. Attach a loop of ribbon through the string to hang the bough on to the door by the neck of the bough – so that the bunch hangs down like a fan. Finish with a piece of wide ribbon around the bunch to cover the string.

Alternatives

*   A bunch of eucalyptus, long stems of rosemary and white-painted twigs will also make a stunning bough.

*   You could add some battery-operated lights to your bough. Make sure the lights are intended for outdoor use.

A novelty Christmas tree for the kitchen

Put a small Christmas tree in a container and decorate it with kitchen utensils like plastic or metal cookie cutters, mini whisks and wooden spoons. You could also add bunches of bright red chillies, herbs and cinnamon sticks. Attach the items to the tree with bows or loops of ribbon.

Alternatives

Add some felt hearts or gingerbread cookies.Finish with garlands of dried apple rings or orange slices threaded on garden string (the hairy kind).

If you want to decorate your office you could adapt this idea by decorating a tree with bits and pieces from the stationery cupboard – garlands of coloured or silver paper clips, bulldog clips tied to the tree with ribbon, rolls of sticky tape, CDs etc.

A topiary tree

These are perfect for a windowsill, a wide mantelpiece or occasional table.

You'll need:

- A small terracotta flowerpot

- A 25cm (10-inch) piece of thick dowelling or a piece of twig the thickness of your thumb

- Damp soil or stone chippings

- A medium-sized foam cone (from the florist)

- Some evergreen small-leaved foliage (bay, eucalyptus, box etc.)

- Kumquats, berries or small decorations

- Glue and glitter (optional)

Fill the flowerpot with damp soil or chippings. Push five centimetres (two inches) of the dowelling or twig into the centre of the base of the cone. Now push the other end into the soil so that the 'tree' is steady. Starting at the bottom of the cone and working around and upwards, completely cover the cone with small sprigs of evergreen.

Now decorate your topiary tree. It's a good idea to use only one kind of decoration and to add just a few so they don't overpower the tree. Perhaps add a few small sprigs of berries, or a few kumquats (push a small length of florists wire through the fruit, twist the wire together, then push the ends of the wire into the cone). Or make a few ribbon bows (pass a piece of wire through the back of the bow, twist and then push the ends of the wire into the cone). Do the same if you want to attach small bunches of berries or small baubles to the tree.

Paint glitter glue on the edges of some of the leaves if you want to give your tree added sparkle.

Alternatives

- You could make a ball-shaped topiary tree by using a longer piece of dowelling or twig and a ball of florists' foam in place of the cone.

- Three miniature topiary trees in a row could be used to decorate your dining table. Use small terracotta cactus pots, a stick of cinnamon to form the trunk, and a small ball of florists' foam for the tree. Use tiny leaves to cover the foam ball and miniature decorations like pearl beads, red ribbon roses or small sprigs of fresh red berries.

Christmas Trees

Real or artificial, the choice is yours, but there is no denying that there is something very special about the unmistakable scent of a real Christmas tree.

Every family has its own idea of what makes the perfectly decorated Christmas tree. For some the tree is an exquisite work of art, or a riot of glorious colour, while for others their tree is a study in minimalist chic, or an annual walk down memory lane through treasured decorations collected year by year.

Buying a tree

Artificial trees – what you should look for

- Look for a tree with well-positioned, densely covered branches.

- Search out a tree with a sturdy base.

- If you buy a tree with fibre-optic lights try to see one working so you can see the effect.

- Buy the best you can afford but beware of becoming a fashion victim. A good artificial tree will last many years but you may soon tire of last year's 'must have' purple tree. So think carefully before rejecting a traditional green tree.

Anthea's Top Tip

If you're decorating a modern flat or a teenage girl's room, buy a white artificial tree and decorate it with baubles in a single colour that reflects the colour of the room. We decorated my fourteen-year-old stepdaughter's room with a white tree and fuchsia-pink baubles. It looked stunning.

Real trees – what you should look for

- Look for needles that are flexible and shiny.

- Check that the needles don't drop off when you pull your hand gently along a branch from the trunk to the tip.

- As a final check, tap the tree. If a shower of needles fall, don't buy it.

If you want to splurge . . . buy a container-grown tree

These will generally be the most expensive – particularly if you want a large tree – but the tree will have all of the roots intact. Try to keep it as cool as possible and well watered. Plant it in the garden after Christmas.

If you want to save . . . buy a cut tree

This will have no roots so when you get it home cut five centimetres (two inches) off the bottom of the trunk so it can take up water. It will need at least two litres a day so make sure your container is large enough to hold the water.

Other kinds of real trees include:

- **A potted tree** – Generally cheaper than a container-grown tree, it will have been dug up just before Christmas and will have suffered disturbance and some root damage. It will also need to be kept as cool as possible and well watered. Plant in the garden after Christmas; if you are lucky it will continue to grow.

- **A root-balled or bare-root tree** – These are sold with the roots wrapped in a net or hessian sack but will have suffered some root damage. You will need to put the tree into a container. It is worth trying to plant the tree in the garden after Christmas but it may not survive.

For more information about buying and caring for Christmas trees take a look at the website of the British Christmas Tree Growers Association (christmastree.org.uk).

Which variety should I buy?

- **Norway spruce** – This is the most widely available tree. It has a good pine scent but the needles can drop quickly in warm conditions.

- **Fraser fir** – A pyramid-shaped tree with blue-green needles. The upward-sweeping branches hold their needles well.

- **Nordmann fir** – A conical-shaped, highly scented fir which holds its needles well.

If you want to splurge

Look out for a Blue Spruce with beautiful dense silver-blue needles. These look sensational but their needles are sharp.

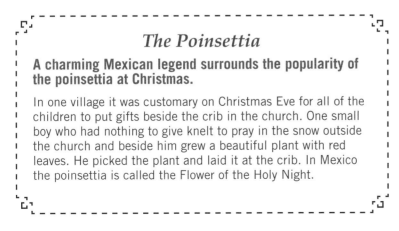

The Poinsettia

A charming Mexican legend surrounds the popularity of the poinsettia at Christmas.

In one village it was customary on Christmas Eve for all of the children to put gifts beside the crib in the church. One small boy who had nothing to give knelt to pray in the snow outside the church and beside him grew a beautiful plant with red leaves. He picked the plant and laid it at the crib. In Mexico the poinsettia is called the Flower of the Holy Night.

Before you buy

Decide where you are going to put the tree, whether it is artificial or real, and check the height and width you have available. (Remember to take a tape measure with you when you buy the tree – don't guess or you might end up having to lop off the tips of the branches or cut a few feet from the tree.)

Inspect the trees on sale from all angles. If it is going to be viewed from all sides you will need it to look perfect all the way round. If you are planning to place it near a wall you can get away with just three good sides, as the other will be hidden.

Avoid trees completely wrapped in nets if you can, as it's impossible to see how dense or well positioned the branches are.

When you take your tree home try to keep it in a garage or shed for a few days before bringing it into the house, to give it time to acclimatise to warmer temperatures. If it is a cut tree, a bare-root or root-balled tree, pot it up into a large sturdy container as soon as possible so that you can start giving it water. If it is a growing tree start watering it every day. Christmas trees are thirsty – particularly in centrally heated houses – so you'll need to water regularly to help prevent needles dropping. Delay buying your tree until the second week of December if you can.

Move the tree into its final location before you start to decorate it. Remember if you are planning to put fairy lights on the tree you will need a socket which can be reached without wires trailing across the floor. Tall trees should be anchored to a wall to ensure they cannot be accidentally knocked over.

If you have to cut any branches from the base of the tree, keep them to use in your decorations.

Anthea's Top Tip

It's a good idea to keep anything dangling or edible off the lower branches of the tree if you have animals or children in the house. They are just too irresistible for words.

Recycle or reuse

If you bought a tree with roots and can't plant it in the garden after Christmas, call your local council to see if they run a recycling scheme. Many will collect trees after the New Year and recycle them into mulch to use in local parks. If you had a cut tree or one that is unlikely to survive, think about chopping it into pieces and piling it into a hidden corner of the garden. It'll provide a valuable haven for beetles, minibeasts, frogs and toads.

Christmas tree safety

If you have pets or small children vacuum or sweep the area around your tree regularly to pick up fallen needles. They can be very sharp and easily pierce tender skin, leading to possible infection. Check your pet's paws regularly.

If you are planning to have lights on a tree outside the house get an electrician to install an external socket. Threading lights through windows or into the garage is not a good idea for safety and security reasons.

Decorating your tree

The Christmas tree is an important focal point so give it the 'wow' factor and let it set the theme for the decorations in the rest of the house.

Tips for a perfect tree:

- Position the tree with its best side facing into the room.

- Decorate the container – this can be as simple or as elaborate as you like. A simple way is to wrap the container in ridged card and tie it with a large paper ribbon bow.

- First add the tree topper – unless you to have a ceremonial placing of the fairy, star or angel at the end of your decorating. (If you leave it to the end there is a chance you will knock other decorations off while reaching up to the top.)

- Starting at the base of the tree weave the lights in and out of the branches, ensuring that the trunk and the middle of the branches are lit. Turn the lights on, stand back and reposition any lights that are hidden.

- If you are using garlands, ribbons, strings of beads or feathers, weave them in and out of the branches.

- Place large decorations at the ends of branches to give impact (large bows, baubles, bells, feather decorations).

- Add smaller decorations to fill in the spaces.

- Stand back from time to time to check the effect.

Buying Christmas lights

Choose lights that have the British Standards Institution Kitemark or conform to BS EN60598-2-20. By law Christmas lights must be 'CE' marked and fitted with a BSI1363 three-pin plug.

Making decorations

Why not make some decorations for your Christmas tree?

Christmas flowers

Make a heart-shaped template using thin card – see page 188 for some templates you can use. Cut out heart shapes in felt or fabric. Take each heart and overstitch round the edges using embroidery thread to give a decorative edge.

Lay eight decorated hearts on a table to form a flower. Join them together at the centre with cotton and attach a shiny button in the middle.

Fix a loop of ribbon to the back of the flower to hang the decoration of the tree.

Christmas hearts

Make some single heart shapes for the Christmas tree as well. (If you want them to look puffy, lightly stuff them.) Add a touch of glamour by decorating the hearts with braid, lace, 'jewels' or sequins.

Make some attractive decorations by threading a selection of varying sized beads onto embroidery silk – a great use for any broken necklaces you have tucked away.

Anthea's Top Tip

If you've used all your decorations and your tree is still looking a little bare, you don't have to rush out to buy some more. Hunt out any bits of old or broken 'bling' – sparkly brooches, earrings, necklaces, buckles and the like – they look fabulous on the tree. The charity shops are a good place to pick up inexpensive pieces. Or look around for matchboxes; wrap them in pretty paper and ribbon to make parcels.

The Christmas tree

Fir trees, decorated with apples, candles, gingerbread and paper flowers were introduced into Britain by German immigrants and then made popular by Queen Victoria's German husband Prince Albert after he erected a decorated tree at Windsor Castle, much to the delight of their children. He also introduced delicate decorations made from spun glass, and miniature wooden toys. Soon decorations were being made commercially.

Decorating your House

Citrus and apple decorations

Dried citrus fruit and apple can be used in a wide variety of ways to make inexpensive decorations. They can be added to wreaths, evergreen swags to drape along mantelpieces and along stairs, used to make decorations or garlands, and to fill vases.

You can dry any kind of citrus fruits such as oranges, limes and lemons.

- Cut the fruit into thin slices (no thinner than half a centimetre). If using apples, soak in lemon juice and salt for two hours, then pat dry with kitchen paper.

- Line baking trays with greaseproof paper and arrange the slices so they are not touching.

- Dry in a low oven (130°C/Gas ½) for six to eight hours, turning regularly.

- To dry whole fruit score the skin from top to bottom at regular intervals so the slits will open during the drying process. Bake until dry.

To make a hanging decoration, thread fruit slices, whole fruit and dried whole spices, such as cinnamon sticks and star anise, on to fishing wire, raffia or string.

Cranberry heart decorations

You can use any combination of these to make the hearts:

- Dried cranberries

- Golden sultanas

- Dark sultanas

- Dried cherries

- Gold or silver beads

You'll also need:

- Some garden wire – the kind used for fencing is ideal (it needs to be malleable but stiff enough to hold its shape)

- A pair of wire-cutters

- A pair of long-nosed pliers

Cut a heart-shaped template in the size that you want from a piece of thin card. Using the template as a guide, bend the wire into a heart shape with the opening at the point of the heart.

Thread dried fruit – and beads if you like – on to the wire, until the wire is completely covered. Twist the ends of the wire together to complete the heart.

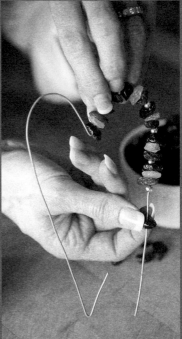

If you've time to spare

Why not make your own Advent calendars?

If you are looking for a change from the usual 'open the window' Advent calendar here are two simple ideas.

Make twenty-five paper cones, write or stick a number on each of them and fill them with small gifts. Get a few identical containers – plant-pot containers are ideal – and put some of the filled cones in each. They look great standing on a windowsill.

Or hang twenty-five dolly pegs over a piece of ribbon or string. Write a number on each and suspend a little wrapped present inside a matchbox from each of the pegs.

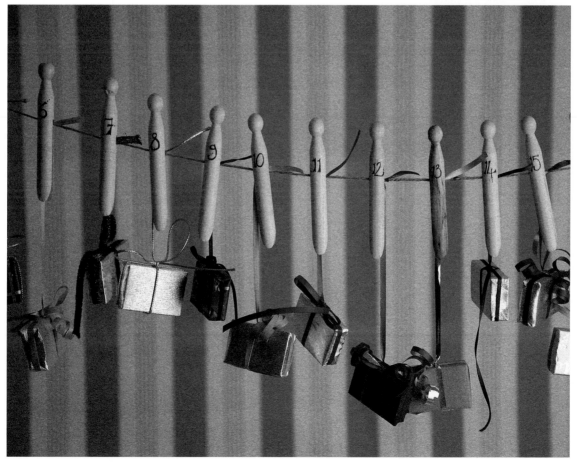

Candle safety

Enjoy the beauty of flickering candlelight at Christmas in safety

- Always keep lighted candles well away from curtains, furniture and soft furnishings. Make sure they are out of draughts.

- Never leave burning candles unattended.

- Make sure any containers you use are stable and cannot be easily knocked over.

- Foliage can become very dry and flammable in centrally heated houses so make sure you don't let candles burn down to the level of the foliage.

- If you make an arrangement of candles always place them on a heatproof base and ensure it is large enough to catch any drips.

- If you plan to light candles in an arrangement make sure each candle is placed at least four centimetres (about two inches) away from the next one or they may melt each other and could topple over.

- Keep candles away from areas used by children and pets.

- Some tea-light holders are made of very flimsy material and may become warm, so don't place them directly on furniture as the heat may scorch the wood. Put them into candle-holders.

If you're short of time

Try these quick fixes to give your home some super-speedy Christmas sparkle.

- Arrange lengths of holly, fir and ivy along your mantelpiece, and place groups of pillar candles among the foliage.

- Bring a scent of spice to your hall. Buy a bag of inexpensive oranges, stud the fruit with cloves and place in an attractive bowl. (If you can place it near a radiator so much the better – the warmth will enhance the scent.)

- Buy pillar candles, glue a circle of bay or ivy leaves around each candle, tie with raffia or ribbon and place in groups around the house. If you plan to light the candles remember to stand them on a heatproof tray or tile or in a container.

Pot plants such as poinsettia, orchids and amaryllis look stunning in the house at Christmas. Or buy a beautiful basket or container of sweet-scented hyacinths, polyanthus and spring bulbs in bloom. Or if you can get organised in time, why not plant up some hyacinth bulbs yourself in late autumn so they are ready to burst into bloom when Christmas arrives.

The meanings of evergreen

Evergreen twigs have been brought into the house at Christmastime for centuries. All had their own special significance.

- *Holly* – the symbol of peace and joy.

- *Ivy* – the sacred plant of Bacchus (the Roman god of wine), said to protect against drunkenness.

- *Mistletoe* – the all-healing plant of peace said to protect homes against thunder and lightning.

- *Bay* – denotes power. Leaves were used in the wreaths worn by Roman poets and heroes.

- *Laurel* – the symbol of purity and honour.

- *Rosemary* – denotes remembrance and friendship.

Pairs or groups of different-sized glass vases filled with shiny apples or dried citrus rings, cones, and nuts in their shells look very elegant.

Or fill baskets with clementines studded with cloves, nutmeg and cinnamon sticks.

If you want to splurge

Create simple arrangements using fresh flowers. You don't have to be an expert flower arranger to make something special. Or order some Christmas arrangements from the florist.

5

With Children in Mind

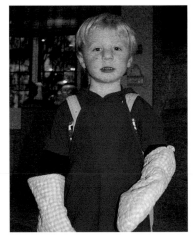

Get the Children Involved

Christmas is an exciting time for children but the days between school ending and Santa arriving can seem awfully long. So try to dream up some ideas to keep their little hands busy and their minds occupied. Make some of them projects they can do on their own when you are busy, and others you can do together. And let them get involved in the Christmas preparations – they'll discover exactly how much Mum has to do to make it such a special time for everyone.

Encourage them to make their own 'to do' list – you're never too young to get into the list-making habit! Suggest that as well as exciting things like making cards, a decoration for the tree or some cookies for Grandma, they could also include helpful tasks like:

- Tidying their bedroom

- Sorting their toys – hopefully, to make room for new ones from Father Christmas. Persuade them to throw away any that are broken and put those they no longer want into a bag to take to a charity shop.

- Tidying their clothes and bagging up anything they don't wear for the charity shop (if Santa sees all those clothes he won't think they need any more!)

- Sorting out their bookshelves

And there are plenty of fun craft and baking ideas.

Decorate their bedroom

Give them a small artificial tree or some bare twigs in a pot and let them decorate it themselves. Be ready for some strange arrangements, but it's theirs and they'll love it. (Real trees in the bedroom are not a great idea as dropped needles are sharp and could injure tender young bare feet.)

Paint a poster

Give them a piece of card, paints, glue and glitter to make a poster to hang on their bedroom door so Santa knows where to call on Christmas Eve.

Make some crispy-cake wreaths

Melt some chocolate in a large bowl and add sufficient puffed-rice cereal to give you a stiff mix. Mix well so all the cereal is coated.

Draw circles on a piece of greaseproof paper and spoon teaspoons of the mixture around the circle to form a knobbly wreath.Place in the fridge to set. Wind ribbon around the wreaths to decorate them.

Hang them on a tree or twig. Or make an edible garland to hang up – but not near the fire or a radiator!

Bake some Christmas cupcakes

Cupcakes are quick and easy to make, and if you don't want to go to the trouble of weighing out ingredients you can pick up a box or packet of cupcake mix from the supermarket. You'll also find a whole range of quick and simple mixes including brownies, flapjacks, cookies, muffins and fairy cakes. Often the packs include decorations but if they don't, buy some sugar-paste Santas, snowmen, holly leaves etc. from the home-baking section, or a couple of tubes of ready-to-use icing.

If you want to make your own, here's a recipe to make twelve cupcakes:

100g/4oz butter or margarine, softened
100g/4oz caster sugar
2 medium eggs
100g/4oz self-raising flour, sieved
1–2tbsp milk
Ready-rolled icing or ready-to-use icing, to decorate

1. Preheat the oven to 190°C/Gas 5. Line a 12-hole cake tin with paper cake cases.

2. Beat the softened butter and sugar together until pale and fluffy. Gradually add the eggs and fold in the sieved flour. Add the milk to the mix until the mixture easily drops off a spoon.

3. Two-thirds fill the cake cases with the mixture.

4. Bake near the top of the oven for 12 to 15 minutes until the cakes are risen, golden and springy to the touch. Place on a wire rack and leave to get cold.

5. Decorate the cakes using ready-rolled icing – it's so quick and easy. Just cut Christmassy shapes using small cookie cutters (or simple stencils), pipe patterns on the cakes with ready-to-use icing in tubes, or pop a sugar-paste Christmas cake decoration on the top.

Shop for presents for the pets

Buy a football sock or welly sock and let the children decorate it and fill it with little gifts for the pets. Or buy a food or drinking bowl and fill it with presents.

Head off for the supermarket or pet store so they can choose the gifts. Set a limit on the cost of filling the stocking – they'll have great fun trying to make the money stretch as far as they can.

Create a card for grandparents or for a special friend

Give the children a box containing some blank cards and envelopes, coloured paper, fabric scraps, lace, ribbon, sequins, scissors, glitter-glue pens and glue and let them create their own masterpieces. If the children are too young to use scissors you'll need to be on hand to help them with any cutting needed. For more ideas for homemade cards see page 25.

Christmas Rocky Road

This recipe is quick, easy and no fuss! Ideal as a treat and great for kids to make as there is no cooking.

Makes 24

400g/14oz good-quality dark chocolate (minimum 70% cocoa)

125g/4½oz butter, softened

4tbsp golden syrup

200g/7oz rich tea biscuits

100g/4oz mini-marshmallows

100g/4oz unglazed cherries

2tsp icing sugar for dusting

1. Slowly melt the chocolate, butter and golden syrup in a saucepan. Scoop out 175ml of the melted mixture and put aside.

2. Break up the rich tea biscuits so you have a mixture of biscuit pieces and crumbs. A good tip is to put the biscuits into a food bag and bash them with your knuckles!

3. Empty the biscuit pieces into the melted chocolate mixture and stir. Then add the marshmallows and cherries.

4. Scoop the mixture into a foil-lined high-edge baking tray (approximately 24cm x 34cm) and level out using a spatula. Pour the reserved 175ml of melted chocolate mixture over the top and smooth out.

5. Refrigerate for a minimum of 2 hours or overnight. Cut into whatever shapes you like – I make slim bars – and dust with icing sugar.

Make a gift for Santa

On Christmas Eve let the children prepare a pretty plate of 'snacks' for Santa and his reindeers. A mince pie, a glass of sherry and a couple of carrots tied with ribbon will be welcomed by the present-laden visitor and his helpers. Did you know that seven million children leave mince pies and a drink for Santa on Christmas Eve?

Anthea's Top Tip

If you don't have children of your own but you have youngsters staying over Christmas, gather together a collection of story books, DVDs, videos, and colouring books and pencils for quiet times.

The great outdoors

- Book a session at a ceramic studio for the whole family. Whether you're artistic or not, you'll all have great fun painting a very individual gift for someone special. My husband took the children and look what I got!

- Take a trip to your nearest town or city to see the Christmas lights and decorations.

- Set up a feeding station for the birds in your garden. Garden birds have a hard time in the winter and need our help. So put out some birdseed, nuts and tasty scraps for them. You'll find books about feeding garden birds in the library.

- Hunt out your nearest ice rink. Some towns have permanent rinks and other temporary rinks are erected in the weeks leading up to Christmas. Go to www.enjoyengland.com/attractions/events to find your nearest rink. Spend a couple of hours on the ice then head for a coffee shop for a steaming hot chocolate and mince pies.

- Choose a crisp day, wrap up warm and head for the local park or out into the country to tramp among the fallen leaves and look for animal tracks.

- Visit a Christmas market or a Christmas fair.

Dear Santa,

We have left you a mince pie and a glass of Sherry to keep you going on the rest of your journey.

Thankyou for stopping by. We have been extra good this year so please leave us lots of presents.

Safe onward trip.
Come back next year!
Lots of Christmas love
A. C + L

6

Gifts from the Kitchen

There is something very special about receiving a gift that someone has taken the trouble to make for you. Pickles, preserves, flavoured vinegars and oils can all be made well in advance and stored away in a cool, dark cupboard to mature (and you can always make an extra jar or two to add to your own Christmas store cupboard). Although cakes, biscuits and sweets need to be made nearer the big day, it really doesn't take long to knock up something scrumptious.

Once again, presentation is important. Use attractive jars and bottles for preserves, vinegar and oils – if you haven't got any suitable jars and bottles you'll find a wide range in cook shops, kitchen sections of large department stores and in charity shops. Add attractive labels and include any advice on using and storage. For example, if you've made a jar of pickles or chutney, make a 'luggage label' style of label and attach it with garden twine. Wire on a couple of red or green chillies to add a splash of colour.

Pack sweets, biscuits and cakes in pretty boxes and bags.

Here are a few quick and easy recipes to try for making your own delicious gifts.

Homemade grainy mustard

Grind two tablespoons of white mustard seeds and two tablespoons of black mustard seeds together in a pestle and mortar. Transfer to a small bowl and add one tablespoon of whole white mustard seeds and one tablespoon of black mustard seeds. Mix to a paste with white-wine vinegar. Add three level teaspoons of clear honey and mix well. Spoon into a small sterilised jar and label.

If you've time to spare

A wicker basket or cardboard box filled with a selection of homemade goodies such as chutney, mustard, chilli flakes, bouquet garni, flavoured oil, flavoured vinegar, vanilla or lavender sugar makes a great gift. If you get some of these made in advance, that'll be one less job to do later.

Or why not make a 'cheese hamper' containing a jar of chutney, some luxury savoury biscuits, a nice piece of cheese (cheat and buy these), and a half-bottle of port or a nice wine. Or an 'Italian hamper' with a pot of chilli flakes, some home-dried herbs, flavoured oil, a packet of pasta (buy this) and a bottle of Italian wine.

Sweet and spicy apple and chilli chutney

Makes 2 to 3 jars

1kg/2¼lb eating apples, peeled, cored and finely chopped

1 onion, peeled and chopped

2 medium-sized chillies, deseeded and chopped

1 clove garlic, chopped

225g/8oz sultanas

50g/2oz prunes

50g/2oz glacé ginger, chopped

500ml/18fl.oz malt vinegar

500g/18oz soft dark brown sugar

2 bay leaves

2tsp ground mixed spice

½tsp Chinese five-spice powder

1tsp turmeric

1tsp salt

1. Place all the ingredients into a large heavy-based saucepan. Cook over a low heat, stirring all the time until the sugar has melted. Bring to the boil, reduce the heat and simmer gently for 1½ to 2 hours or until the chutney has thickened. Remove the bay leaves.

2. Spoon the hot chutney into warmed sterilised jars and seal immediately.

3. Make an attractive label and attach it to the neck of the jar with a piece of red and white checked ribbon. Write the name of the chutney on one side of the label and on the other side write: 'Store in a cool dry place. After opening keep in the refrigerator. Use within six months.'

To sterilise bottles and jars

Preheat the oven to 150°C/ Gas 2. Wash the bottles in hot soapy water, rinse and dry well. Line a baking tray with kitchen towel and stand or lay the bottles on the tray. Place in the oven for fifteen minutes. Remove from the oven and allow to cool slightly before filling them.

NOTE: Use plastic or cork tops for flavoured vinegars, as vinegar will eat into metal tops.

Spicy Christmas chutney

Makes 6 jars

1½kg/3½lb cooking apples, peeled, cored and sliced

1kg/2¼lb onion, peeled and finely chopped

450g/1lb sultanas

1.2 litres/2 pints malt vinegar

450g/1lb cranberries (fresh or frozen)

700g/1½lb dark soft brown sugar

2tbsp black treacle

2tsp ground ginger

1tsp salt

2tsp cinnamon

2tsp mixed spice

1½tbsp mixed pickling spice (tied in a small piece of muslin or thin white cloth)

1. Place the prepared apple, onions and sultanas into a large saucepan or preserving pan.

2. Add half of the vinegar and simmer for 30 minutes.

3. Mix in the remaining ingredients and the other half of the vinegar and simmer, stirring all the time until the sugar has dissolved.

4. Simmer the chutney until it acquires a jam-like consistency, stirring frequently to ensure it does not burn.

5. Place in sterilised jars. Add festive labels and store in a cool dry place until needed.

Vinegars and oils

Flavoured oils and vinegars are delicious but expensive to buy. You can make your own for a fraction of the cost.

Use attractive bottles to turn them into desirable gifts for 'foodie' friends.

Flavoured vinegars

A variety of herbs and fruits can be added to vinegar to provide a range of subtle flavours.

Here is a basic method:

1. Place 700ml (1½ pints) of vinegar into a saucepan. Bring to the boil and boil for two minutes. Remove from the heat and cool.

2. Wash the herbs/spices/fruits you are using and allow to dry. Divide them between the sterilised bottles. Pour over the warm vinegar. Seal the bottles and label.

Salad vinegar

(Use to make salad dressings and vinaigrettes)

3 sprigs of thyme

2 small fresh red chillies (optional)

2 medium cloves garlic

1tsp black peppercorns

700ml/1½ pints white-wine vinegar

Lemon vinegar

Rind of 3 lemons, thinly pared to avoid the white pith

700ml/1½ pints distilled vinegar

Thyme and rosemary vinegar

4 sprigs thyme

2 sprigs rosemary

2 strips lemon peel

700ml/1½ pints cider vinegar

Raspberry vinegar

50g washed fresh raspberries

½tsp black peppercorns

700ml/1½ pints white-wine vinegar

Flavoured oils

These are delicious used in cooking and to drizzle over salads.

Lemon and coriander oil

Put two teaspoons of coriander seeds and a few strips of thinly pared lemon rind into a sterilised bottle and fill with olive oil. Seal.

Chilli oil

Thread four or five small chillies onto a wooden skewer. Put into a sterilised bottle and fill with olive oil. Seal.

Garlic oil

Thread five garlic cloves onto a wooden skewer. Put into a sterilised bottle and fill with olive oil. Seal.

Label the oils and store in a cool, dark place, as they can deteriorate when exposed to light.

Oversized simple labels look very attractive hanging from the necks of bottles of oil and vinegar. Write the name of the vinegar or oil on it, and perhaps a recipe suggestion on the back.

Flavoured sugars

Vanilla and lavender sugars are ideal for adding to desserts, pancakes, muffins, rice puddings and custards.

To make vanilla sugar, fill a lidded glass container with caster sugar and push two vanilla pods into the sugar.

To make lavender sugar, which has a very subtle flavour, add a few sprigs of lavender to a lidded glass container filled with caster sugar.

Flapjacks

Makes 16 to 20 slices

225g/8oz of butter
150g/5oz demerara sugar
3tbsp golden syrup
400g/14oz porridge oats
150g/5oz desiccated coconut

1. Preheat the oven to 170°C/Gas 3 and line a 20cm (8-inch) square baking tin with baking parchment.

2. Over a low heat melt the butter, demerara sugar and golden syrup together in a large saucepan.

3. Add the porridge oats and desiccated coconut and mix well together. Spoon into the prepared tin and level the top. Bake in the preheated oven until golden brown and firm to the touch.

4. Cool and cut into squares.

If you want to save money

Batches of Christmas biscuits, biscotti, muffins, smart cupcakes and sweets are all quick to make. Spend an hour in the kitchen and you'll have a batch of presents for far less than they would cost to buy.

Just pop them into simple paper bags, tie the neck with string and add a pretty home-made label. Or arrange them in a pretty box lined with greaseproof paper.

Almond biscuits

Another gift that goes well with a bottle of wine

Makes 20–24

300g/11oz plain flour, sieved

150g/6oz icing sugar, sifted

25g/1oz ground almonds

150g/6oz butter, cut into small pieces

1 large egg

1tsp almond extract

1tbsp water

Caster sugar to finish

1. Preheat the oven to 180°C/Gas 4. Line baking trays with parchment.

2. Put the flour, icing sugar and almonds into a mixing bowl and mix together. Add the butter and rub into the dry ingredients until the mixture resembles fine breadcrumbs.

3. Add the egg, almond extract and water and use a fork to mix together into a dough. Wrap in clingfilm and chill until firm.

4. Lightly flour a pastry board or clean work surface and roll out the dough until it is 3mm (⅛ inch) thick.

5. Use cookie cutters to cut out biscuits and place on the baking sheets. Sprinkle lightly with caster sugar and bake for 10 to 15 minutes until the biscuits are lightly browned.

6. Leave to cool on a wire rack. Store in an airtight tin.

> **If the children need little gifts for their friends why not buy a couple of packets of cookie mix and let them make giant cookies decorated with mini sweets. Make a hole through each biscuit with a skewer before baking them. When they are cold thread a piece of ribbon through the hole and attach a gift card for a message.**

Mini chocolate and hazelnut biscotti

A 'dunking' treat for chocoholics and coffee lovers!

Makes 16

225g/8oz plain flour

1tsp baking powder

225g/8oz caster sugar

6tbsp cocoa powder

2 medium eggs

75g/3oz hazelnuts

1. Preheat the oven to 180°C/Gas 4.

2. Sieve the flour into a mixing bowl and add the baking powder, sugar and cocoa. Lightly beat the eggs and add to the dry ingredients. Mix together well then fold in the hazelnuts.

3. Remove the dough from the bowl and divide into two pieces. Roll each piece into a flat sausage shape, about 4cm (1½ inches) high. Place on a sheet of baking parchment on a baking tray and flatten slightly with your fingers. Bake for 25 to 30 minutes until firm. Remove from the oven.

4. Allow to cool for 10 minutes then slice each of the rolls into 1cm (½ inch) slices. Place the slices back on to the baking tray and bake for a further 10 to 15 minutes. Remove from the oven and cool on a rack.

Stored in an airtight container, with a couple of sugar lumps to absorb moisture, the biscuits will keep crisp for two to three weeks.

To give as a gift put them in a cellophane bag and tie a ribbon and a label round the neck.

If you're short of time

If you aren't confident in the kitchen or simply short of time, don't despair – you can 'cheat' a little. Head for the local farmers' market, farm shop or W.I. market where you're sure to find some good-quality home-made bakes and preserves. You can always 'pretty up' the packaging, to give them a personal touch.

If you want to splurge

You'll find a wide range of ready-made food hampers in supermarkets, fine-food stores and at the deli in the weeks leading up to Christmas. It's also worth tracking down specialist companies that make luxury hampers on the Internet. If you want something really individual, some companies and fine-food stores will let you select products to go into a hamper and then make it up for you.

Whisky truffles

Makes about 20 truffles

200g/7oz good-quality dark chocolate, chopped

55ml/2fl.oz double cream

25g/1oz butter

50g/2oz chocolate-cake crumbs

2tsp whisky

Dark-chocolate sprinkles, cocoa powder or drinking-chocolate powder, to decorate

1. Place the chopped chocolate in a medium heatproof bowl.

2. Put the cream and butter in a small nonstick saucepan and heat over a low heat, stirring all the time until the mixture is just boiling. Add the cream mixture to the chocolate and stir until the mixture is smooth and the chocolate has completely melted.

3. Stir in the cake crumbs and the whisky. Refrigerate until the mixture is firm. Take heaped teaspoonfuls of the truffle mixture and roll into balls.

4. To decorate, roll the truffles in chocolate sprinkles, cocoa powder or drinking-chocolate powder.

5. Place the truffles on a flat plate and return to the fridge to become firm. Pop into foil or paper sweet cases.

Rum, brandy or vodka can be used instead of whisky. The truffles will keep in the fridge for a week.

Christmas muffins

Makes 12

12 paper muffin cases
275g/10oz plain flour
2tsp baking powder
½tsp bicarbonate of soda
½tsp salt
75g/3oz caster sugar
1 large egg
200ml/7fl.oz milk
90ml/3fl.oz vegetable oil
350g/12oz sweet mincemeat (preferably vegetarian)
50g/2oz chopped walnuts or pecans
Icing sugar, to decorate

1. Preheat oven to 190°C/Gas 5. Place muffin cases in a deep muffin tin.

2. Sift together the flour, baking powder, bicarbonate of soda and salt into a mixing bowl. Stir in the sugar. In a separate bowl, lightly beat the egg with a fork and stir in the milk, oil and mincemeat.

3. Pour the egg mixture into the flour mixture and add the nuts. Stir the mixture together. Do not over-mix. The batter should be lumpy but there should be no flour visible.

4. Spoon the mixture into the muffin cases until they are three-quarters full.

5. Bake in the preheated oven for 20 to 25 minutes until the muffins are well risen and lightly browned. Place on a wire rack to cool. When the muffins are completely cold, dust with icing sugar.

If you want to save money

If you're short of cash, here's a novel gift – a batch of freshly baked Christmas muffins in a muffin tray.

Buy a six- or twelve-hole muffin tin and bake a batch of Christmas muffins (using muffin cases) in the tin. Place the muffins in their cases on a wire rack and allow to get cold. Wash and dry the tin, and pop the muffins back in the tin.

When they are completely cold, wrap the muffins and the tin in cellophane paper and tie with ribbon.

You could do the same using a bun tray filled with mince pies dusted with icing sugar, or decorated cup cakes.

7

All Wrapped Up

Gift-wrapping

With the amazing array of papers and trimmings available it's easy to make your gifts extra special. All you need is a little time and some imagination.

Mix and match colours and textures, and add finishing touches with ribbons, feathers, artificial sprigs of berries, pearls, paper flowers, small Christmas tree decorations and shiny baubles.

Or if you want to opt for a natural look use plain or brown textured paper with dried seed heads, plaited raffia, dried orange rings, cinnamon sticks and pressed leaves.

Add glamour to your gifts

- Wrap your parcel in brown paper. Wrap several strands of raffia round the parcel one way, and tie with a knot so that you have several raffia ends. Wrap wired voile ribbon round the parcel the other way and tie with a bow. Wire a bunch of cinnamon sticks and a couple of dried orange slices under the bow.

- Here's one for the boys, if you're reading this. Wrap your parcel in brown or white paper. Wrap a piece of ribbon around the longest sides of the parcel overlapping the ends on the underside and securing with sticky tape. Just before giving the present slip a sin-gle fresh rosebud under the ribbon. She'll be impressed!

- Add impact to a simply wrapped gift by thread-ing an old diamante buckle on to a piece of ribbon.

Christmas stockings

According to legend, the tradition of hanging up stockings on Christmas Eve dates from a deed of kindness by St Nicholas, the patron saint of children. As a Christmas gift for three poor children he dropped coins down their chimney. The coins fell into their stockings, hanging over the fire to warm. Since that time hanging up a stocking on Christmas Eve is said to bring prosperity.

Wrapping tips

- A festive paper tablecloth is ideal for wrapping large boxes and unusual-shaped presents.

- If you have a present which is too bulky to wrap, increase the excitement by wrapping a small gift associated with the large present – for example a bicycle bell or helmet if the main present is a shiny new bike. Place a clue in the small gift leading to the location of the larger present. Put the small box under the Christmas tree and the large present in the garage, a shed or another room in the house decorated with balloons, streamers and a big bow.

- To make bows that hold their shape use wired voile or organza ribbon.

- Transform plain paper by using stencils and stamps. Or dip a small piece of sponge in gold paint and dab onto the paper.

- If you're handy with the sewing machine you can whip up a quick sack for a bulky present from a remnant of fabric. Tie the neck with a large bow and attach a homemade oversized gift label.

- To remove the tight folds from sheets of tissue paper, iron with a warm iron (no steam).

If you're short of time

Buy a selection of different-sized gift bags and some packets of tissue paper. Lay your gifts in the centre of two pieces of tissue paper, gather up the edges and tie the neck with pretty string. Pop it in the bag, so that the 'tissue paper wings' peep out of the top. You can personalise the bags by adding a big bow and a sprig of evergreen and berries, a small Christmas tree decoration, sequins or shapes cut out from old Christmas cards.

Wrapping an awkward-shaped present

Get a piece of cellophane paper and lay it on a table. Place a piece of matching or contrasting tissue paper on top at an angle, and top with another piece of cellophane, again placed at an angle.

Put the gift in the centre and pull up the wrapping to enclose it. Squeeze the paper together above the gift and secure with a bow. Fan out the points.

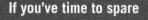

If you've time to spare

Check out craft shops and Further Education centres for present wrapping and decorating classes. Many run half-day and one-day courses in the weeks before Christmas. November and December issues of magazines are also a good place to look for inspiration.

Get it gift-wrapped

If you're short of time or your gift-wrapping isn't up to scratch, make use of the gift-wrapping services in many stores at Christmas (in some places the service is free but you have to ask). You might also be lucky enough to find a charity stall set up in a shopping centre offering a gift-wrapping service in return for a donation to the charity.

Some Internet companies offer a gift-wrapping service – so make use of it when you buy from them.

Gifts under the tree

A collection of beautifully wrapped presents under the tree adds to the anticipation of Christmas morning. So be imaginative with your wrapping.

Create a theme to match the colour and style of your Christmas tree decorations so they form part of the overall picture.

- If you've opted for traditional red and gold then continue the theme by wrapping all of the presents in gold or red paper, with elaborate ribbons and bows in a rich dark green, red or gold.

- If you've chosen a rustic look for your decorations with natural decorations, cones, bows, candy walking sticks and gingerbread, try wrapping your gifts in a simple Shaker style.

- Icy-white, silver and blue has become a popular Christmas colour scheme. To co-ordinate with this, wrap your gifts in icy-white and silver paper and decorate them with sparkly ribbons, 'frost'-dusted flowers and sprays of silver beads.

Make your own gift labels

Stylish handmade gift tags add the finishing touch to any beautifully wrapped present.

Experiment with different natural papers and card to make your labels. Let your imagination run riot and decorate them with embossed images, tissue leaves, stencils, stamps, cut-out shapes, gold or silver foil leaves or gold thread.

Here are a few ideas:

- Cut out holly leaves from rough hand-made paper. Outline the leaves using a gold pen, punch a hole and attach a ribbon.

- Make a label from a dark-coloured card, then stick a dried flower head or tissue leaf on the label. Attach ribbon or string to tie.

- Stick a gold-foil leaf on to a square of card. Add gold ribbon to tie.

- Save time making labels by buying a packet of luggage tags and decorating them.

- Buy packets of festive card-making 'bits and pieces' and use them to decorate your labels.

- Use cut-outs from old Christmas cards.

Anthea's Top Tips

Turn gift-wrapping into an event. Get yourself a plateful of nibbles; pour a nice glass of wine. Gather up your wrapping paper, ribbons, accessories, sticky tape and scissors on a large table. Put on a CD of carols to get you in the mood and start wrapping.

Keep all your gift labels, ribbons, string, bows, trimmings, scissors, sticky tape and pens in a box so all the family knows where to find them.

Christmas crackers

Everyone loves Christmas crackers – even though the contents can be predictable and the jokes awful! There is a bewildering selection of Christmas crackers on sale in shops and on the Internet so it's not too difficult to find some to perfectly complement your Christmas table.

If you want to save money

Crackers at the lower end of the price range can be disappointing, so why not make an alternative – something that's 'all your own work'? They needn't take long to make.

- Hunt out a remnant of organza, silk or voile. Cut it into squares. Wrap a tiny gift in tissue and place in the centre of each square. Gather up the corners and tie a ribbon around the neck. Trim to match your table decorations.

- If you've opted for a natural look for your table, get a piece of hessian. Cut it into squares and fray the edges. Pop a gift in the centre, gather up the fabric and tie with raffia or garden string. Decorate with a spray of evergreen and some berries or tiny fir cones.

If you want to splurge

If money is no object you can find beautiful and original crackers in major department stores and from specialist websites. If you decide to order online, get your order in early as many of the crackers are hand-made and may quickly sell out.

Making crackers

Making your own crackers is great fun and gives you the chance to choose individual gifts. But it can be time-consuming if you are designing and making them from scratch, especially as you have to track down everything you need before you can start. An alternative is to look for a basic 'cracker kit' and then decorate them yourself. You'll find them on the Internet and also at large craft and hobby shops. Another option is to buy pre-rolled crackers, which you can put your own gifts in.

If you enjoy making crackers don't forget to keep your eyes open for glitzy trimmings and ribbons in the remnant boxes in haberdashery departments and craft stores. It's also worth making a visit to a Christmas craft fair for inspiration.

Decorating crackers

Decorate your crackers to match your Christmas table with ribbon, bows, lace, glitter, stars, feathers, glitter-glue, self-adhesive 'jewels' or stencils. Buy yourself a glue gun to make life easier.

Slip in a gift, and a joke and hat (many kits come complete with these) if you like. Attach sticky labels with your guests' names and they double as place settings.

Cracker fillers and table presents

How many key rings, miniature packs of playing cards, spinning tops and metal puzzles can anyone possibly want? If you make your own 'crackers' you can be much more imaginative.

Here are some ideas for cracker fillers and table presents:

- Trial sizes of perfume and classy cosmetics

- Instant lottery cards. Or a lottery ticket for the next big draw – who could resist the chance of being a millionaire by the New Year!

- Miniature bottles of liqueurs

- Bosk tokens or music vouchers

- A small item to match the person's interests or hobbies.

- Slip a 'promise' in each cracker instead of a gift – a promise of an evening's baby-sitting, an ironing session, a car wash … or something else!

Anthea's Top Tip

What about buying a cracker with a wrapping you can 'plant' in the garden instead of tossing in the bin? The attractive Biome Lifestyle crackers are made of hand-made paper embedded with wild flower seeds. So when you've pulled the cracker all you have to do is lay the wrapper on the ground, cover it with soil and wait for a host of beautiful wild flowers to appear. If you want to know more go to www.biomelifestyle.com.

Christmas crackers

In 1847, confectioner's apprentice Tom Smith was peering in the windows of sweet shops in Paris looking for inspiration. His eyes fell on sugared almonds wrapped in twists of tissue paper.

He rushed home and introduced the British public to the fascinating 'bon-bons'. They sold well at Christmas but demand quickly fell off after the festive season. Tom decided to capitalise on the seasonal appeal and soon added kiss mottoes (love messages), jokes and small toys to the almond in the wrapper. But still, he decided, something was missing. Then one winter evening sitting by the fire he listened to the crackling of his roaring log fire. After two years of experiment he had perfected the saltpetre strip – and the cracker's banger had arrived.

Make your posting first class

Don't let your Christmas gifts end their journey at Royal Mail's 'heartbreak hotel'. Each year thousands of Christmas parcels fail to reach their destination or arrive damaged because they are badly wrapped or incorrectly addressed.

Unbreakable gifts

Even soft gifts like scarves and gloves need protection if you are posting them. Wrapping them in gift-wrap and then brown paper is not sufficient, as the paper can easily be torn. Place the wrapped present inside a padded envelope, a lightweight box or a piece of corrugated paper and then wrapping paper. You can also buy special 'flat-pack' lightweight posting boxes in a variety of sizes from most Post Offices, office suppliers and high-street stationers. The boxes take only seconds to make up and all you have to do is pop your wrapped presents in, secure with parcel tape and string, and address them.

Fragile items

The safest method is to put the gift in a box (if it isn't already in one) and then gift-wrap it. Then put the wrapped box into another box that is at least five centimetres (two inches) larger all round than the gift. Pad underneath the gift, and round all of the sides and on top, with bubble wrap, shredded paper or polystyrene beads. The present should not be able to move around and should be well cushioned on all sides. Close the box securely with sticky tape and wrap in strong brown paper. Secure your parcel with parcel tape and string.

CDs and DVDs need more protection than just their plastic container. If they aren't sufficiently cushioned there is a danger that the plastic will crack and may scratch the CD. You can buy a special ridged cardboard box designed for posting them, or wrap the disc and its case with sufficient bubble wrap to go round three times. Secure the bubble wrap with sticky tape and place in a padded envelope or box.

Don't be tempted to guess the weight of a small parcel so you can pop it into the post box and avoid queuing to have it weighed. If you don't put sufficient stamps on a parcel it could be delayed – and the recipient may have to pay a surcharge.

Remember, with the pricing system used by Royal Mail cards have to be no larger than 24cm by 16.5cm and 0.5cm thick to qualify as a 'letter'. They also have to weigh less than 60g. Cards larger than this are classed as a 'large letter' and cost more than the normal first- and second-class letter rate.

Addressing parcels

Write the name of the recipient in block capitals and always include the postcode. The postcodes for addresses in the UK can be found at www.royalmail.com.

Write the word 'sender', your name and full address (including the postcode) on the side of the parcel, so it can be returned to you if it can't be delivered.

Posting parcels overseas

There are restrictions on what can be sent overseas and regulations vary from country to country. Before you post any parcels abroad to family and friends always check by visiting www.royalmail.com, as international posting regulations do change from time to time. Check carefully where on the parcel you should write the recipient's name and address and where you should write your name and address. Also check whether you need a customs clearance form. They are necessary for some countries but not for others. If your parcel should have a form, but arrives without one, it will be sent straight back to you. Also remember to check the last posting dates for Christmas. Try not to leave your parcel posting until the last minute to avoid wasting time in long queues.

Spending Christmas overseas

If you are spending Christmas abroad and plan to take presents with you, don't wrap them before you go – you may be told to unwrap them for a customs inspection! Take along wrapping paper, tape, ribbons and labels and wrap them when you arrive.

Always check in the customs section on the website of the country you are visiting to make sure that you are allowed to take the gifts you have bought into the country. Countries may have restrictions on certain items.

8

Freezing and Making Ahead

Your freezer is your greatest ally at Christmas, so make it work for you. In November give it a good clear-out and if it resembles an ice cave, defrost it – you'll need every inch of freezer space you can get. Make a list of everything as you put it back and resolve to use as much of the food as you can before Christmas – it'll save you money and time.

When you've decided on your Christmas menus, mark all those dishes or parts of dishes that can be made in advance and frozen, and set aside some time in the kitchen. Also buy any frozen food you plan to use as soon as it appears in the shops so you can snap up any early-bird bargains.

If there's space in the freezer try to make or buy some meals you can whip out to feed the family when you're short of time.

You can get many of your Christmas Day 'essentials' and food for entertaining squirrelled away in the freezer weeks in advance.

- Cook stuffings and freeze them ready to reheat and serve (if you can't manage that, just freezing the breadcrumbs is a great timesaver).

- Cook sauces (such as bread sauce and cranberry sauce) and freeze ahead.

- Make and freeze brandy butter.

- Make or buy and freeze mince pies.

- Prepare and freeze desserts.

Buying in

If you've decided to buy in all your Christmas food get started early and make as much use as you can of the freezer. Check that dishes you buy are suitable for freezing.

Packaging on ready prepared dishes and accompaniments can be pretty bulky and take up valuable space. If freezer space is tight remove outer packaging (unless the items are fragile), slip into a freezer bag and label. Don't forget to keep the cooking/reheating instructions.

Food for the freezer

Cranberry sauce

Serves 6 to 8

Juice of 3 small oranges
Zest of 1 orange
350g/12oz fresh cranberries (or frozen, thawed)
2tbsp clear honey
1tbsp thin-cut marmalade
150ml/5fl.oz port

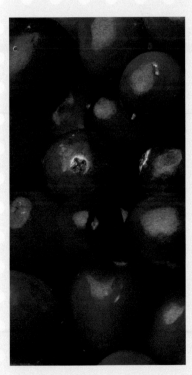

1. Put all the ingredients into a saucepan. Bring to the boil and simmer, uncovered, for 25 minutes.

2. Remove half of the cranberries using a slotted spoon. Place in a blender and whiz until smooth. Return to the pan and mix well. Taste and add additional honey if needed.

3. Cool. Place in a suitable container and freeze. Thaw overnight in the fridge when needed.

Under wraps

Pack food well before freezing. You need to keep as much air out as possible and prevent moisture loss. Use freezer bags – they are tougher than normal food bags. Squeeze out excess air and secure with freezer ties or plastic clips. Label the food before you put it into the freezer. Remember to include a date on the label.

Bread sauce

Serves 6 to 8

1 onion, quartered and studded with 6 cloves
2 bay leaves
600ml/1pint milk
110g/4oz fresh white breadcrumbs
Salt and pepper

To finish
4tbsp double cream
25g/1oz butter
Freshly grated nutmeg

1. Put the onion quarters studded with cloves and the bay leaves
    into a nonstick saucepan and pour over the milk. Bring to the
    boil. Turn off the heat and leave to infuse for an hour.

2. Remove the onion and the bay leaves. (If you prefer a more
    intense onion flavour, chop half of the onion finely and put back
    into the saucepan.) Add the breadcrumbs and bring to the boil.
    Simmer gently, stirring, for 6 to 8 minutes. Season with salt and
    pepper.

3. Allow the sauce to cool and place in a freezer-proof container.
    Freeze for up to a month.

To serve: Defrost overnight. Place in a saucepan with the double
cream, butter and a light sprinkling of freshly grated nutmeg. Heat
through and serve.

Brandy butter

Serves 6 to 8

110g/4oz unsalted butter, softened
Finely grated zest of 1 orange or mandarin
50ml/2fl.oz brandy
350g/12oz icing sugar

1. Put the butter, half of the icing sugar and the orange or mandarin zest into a mixing bowl and beat together until smooth. Add the remaining sugar and the brandy.

2. Transfer to a freezer-proof container and freeze for up to a month.

To serve: Transfer the brandy butter to a serving dish and use a fork to make it into a cone shape. Float a little brandy around the edge to form a moat. Decorate the cone with slivers of almond, if you like.

Ring the changes by replacing the brandy with rum, whisky or Cointreau.

Apple and cranberry stuffing

Serves 8

2tbsp oil

4 eating apples, peeled, cored and finely chopped

1 medium onion, peeled and finely chopped

3tbsp fresh thyme leaves

700g/1½lb pork sausage meat (or sausages removed from their skins)

175g/6oz fresh wholemeal breadcrumbs

1 egg, beaten

Salt and freshly ground black pepper

200g/7oz fresh or frozen cranberries

1. Heat the oil in a nonstick frying pan and cook the apples and onion slowly until softened. Transfer to a mixing bowl. Add the remaining ingredients, except the cranberries, and mix together using your hands. Season with salt and pepper and stir in the cranberries.

2. Use the stuffing to fill the neck of the turkey or transfer to a greased and lined square baking tin, brush with a little melted butter, and bake in a moderate oven (180°C/Gas 4) for 30 to 35 minutes or until the stuffing is firm and the sausage meat cooked.

3. Allow to cool slightly and then cut into squares if you cooked it in a tin.

4. The stuffing can be made ahead and then frozen for up to a month.

To serve: Reheat in the oven until piping hot.

Remember to make enough so that you have some stuffing to serve on Boxing Day and in turkey sandwiches!

Stuffings

You can make your stuffings in advance, buy some ready-made that can be frozen, or if you prefer make them from dry ingredients nearer the day.

Mushroom and chestnut stuffing

A vegetarian alternative

Serves 6 to 8

2tbsp oil
8 shallots
200g/7oz button mushrooms, chopped
175g/6oz chestnuts (ready-cooked, vacuum-packed or in a jar), chopped
4tbsp fresh sage, chopped
200g/7oz fresh wholemeal breadcrumbs
1 large egg plus 1 egg yolk
Salt and freshly ground black pepper

1. Heat the oil in a nonstick frying pan and cook the shallots and
    the mushrooms for 3 to 5 minutes until they have softened.
    Allow to cool.

2. Place the remaining ingredients in a mixing bowl, add the
    shallots and mushrooms and mix well together. Season with salt
    and pepper.

3. Press the stuffing into a lightly greased square baking tin or
    shallow ovenproof dish and bake in a moderate oven (180°C/Gas
    4) for 20 to 25 minutes until the stuffing is golden and firm. Cut
    into squares.

The stuffing can be made ahead and stored in the freezer or cooked
the day before, stored in the fridge and reheated in the oven.

Ice cream surprise

The perfect end to any festive meal – or as an
alternative to Christmas pudding

Serves 6

6 luxury shortcrust pastry mince pies
2tbsp brandy (optional)
500ml/18fl.oz tub good-quality vanilla ice cream

To serve
Chopped walnuts
Luxury caramel sauce (ready-made in a tub or jar)

1. Crumble the mince pies into a large mixing bowl and add the
    brandy (if using). Add the tub of ice cream and mix gently, until
    combined. Place in a freezer-proof container and refreeze for
    at least 2 hours. Remove from the freezer 10 minutes before
    serving.

To serve: place two good-sized scoops of the ice cream into
attractive glasses or serving bowls. Drizzle over the caramel sauce
and sprinkle with chopped walnuts.

Raspberries and iced crème fraîche

Simple but sensational

Serves 6

500g/18oz full-fat crème fraîche

175g/6oz icing sugar

4tbsp rum, vodka or brandy

To serve

Raspberry coulis, raspberries, chocolate curls, icing sugar and mint leaves

1. Line a 450g/1lb loaf tin with clingfilm.

2. Place the crème fraîche, icing sugar and spirit into a large bowl and whisk until the mixture thickens slightly. Pour into the loaf tin. Cover the top with clingfilm and freeze until needed (it will keep for up to a month).

To serve: place a slice of the iced crème fraîche on to a flat side plate. Drizzle raspberry coulis (from a jar or bottle) around the plate. Arrange raspberries over the iced crème fraîche. Place a small mound of dark chocolate curls at one side. Sprinkle with icing sugar and decorate with a pair of mint leaves.

As an alternative, you could substitute a good-quality chocolate sauce for the raspberry coulis, use small cubes of fresh mango instead of raspberries, and make a small mound of toasted slivered almonds instead of chocolate curls.

> **Tip**
> Cut cheesecakes, gateaux, tortes and tarts into slices while they are still slightly frozen – you'll get neat, even slices

A traditional Christmas pudding

A perfect pudding that works every time

Serves 8

1 cooking apple, peeled, cored and coarsely grated

1 medium carrot, peeled and coarsely grated

175g/6oz seedless raisins

175g/6oz sultanas

110g/4oz currants

110/4oz prunes, coarsely chopped

25g/1oz chopped mixed peel

25g/1oz chopped nuts

Finely grated rind of 1 orange

Juice of 1 orange

150ml/5fl.oz port or ruby wine

110g/4oz butter, softened

225g/8oz soft dark brown sugar

½tsp cinnamon

¼tsp nutmeg

1tsp mixed spice

2 eggs

110g/4oz self-raising flour

150ml/5fl.oz rum, brandy or sherry

110g/4oz fresh wholemeal or white breadcrumbs

1tbsp black treacle

1. Soak the fruit, grated carrot, nuts, orange rind and orange juice for 1 or 2 days in port or ruby wine.

2. Take a 1.2-litre/2-pint pudding basin (or two 600ml/1-pint basins) and cut a small disk of greaseproof paper to fit the base of the basin. Grease the basin with a little butter.

3. Cream the butter and sugar together in a large mixing bowl. Beat in the spices, eggs and flour. Stir in the remaining ingredients.

4. Turn the mixture into the prepared basin and level the top.

5. Make a pleat in a sheet of buttered greaseproof paper and lay over the top of the basin. Tie the paper over the basin with a piece of thin string. Cover the basin with a pudding cloth and tie with another piece of string. Tie a piece of string across the basin to make it easy to lift out when the pudding is cooked.

6. Place the basin in a steamer, cover and steam for 6 hours. Remember to top up the steamer at regular intervals with boiling water (a few slices of lemon in the steaming water will prevent your steamer from becoming stained). If you haven't got a steamer use a large lidded saucepan (stand the pudding on an old saucer).

9

Christmas Baking

Christmas Cakes

Christmas cakes, mince pies, sweet treats and festive biscuits are all part of the celebrations. But, unless you enjoy baking and have the time, you don't have to make them yourself. The supermarkets and bakeries are filled with a mouth-watering array of festive goodies.

If you do want to bake your own teatime you'll find plenty of tips and ideas in this chapter.

Three quick ways to decorate a Christmas cake

Make or buy an un-iced Christmas cake, cover it with marzipan and ready-to-roll icing and decorate in one of these simple ways. Alternatively you could buy a plain iced cake, and use one of our ideas to pretty it up.

If you're short of time

If you need a special cake in a hurry buy a luxury cake mix – there are loads in the super-market – and give it some festive decorations. Or leave it plain and dust with icing sugar.

- Buy a length of white beaded trimming and wrap around the cake, securing it with a long coloured-headed pin or with sticky tape. Place a matching bow to conceal the join. Then just before serving lay a half-opened red rosebud across the top of the cake and dust lightly with icing sugar.

- Place the cake on a cake board or cake stand. Wrap a length of ribbon around the side of the cake. Using a sheet of ready-rolled icing cut out twenty holly or ivy leaves using a cutter. Lay a couple of wine bottles on your work surface (or a couple of rolling pins), and lay the leaf shapes over the bottles to dry, so they dry in a curved shape. Also make some tiny holly berries from the icing. Put a tablespoon of icing sugar into a small bowl and mix to a soft paste with a little water. Dip the ends of the dried leaves into the paste and arrange in pairs round the edge of the top of the cake. Take a cocktail stick and place tiny blobs of icing on the cake wherever you want to place three or four berries (between each pair of leaves).

- Wrap a lemon-yellow or green voile ribbon around the edge of the cake and attach a bow at the join. Place on a cake board or cake stand. Decorate the centre of the cake with sugared fruits. Use only small fruits which have their skins intact so they don't bleed juices on to the icing – e.g. red and green grapes, kumquats and cherries, with stalks if possible.

- Sugar the fruits by washing and drying them thoroughly on kitchen towel. Lightly beat an egg white with a fork, then dip the fruit in the egg white and then into caster sugar. Dry on baking parchment so they don't stick. Arrange them in the centre of the cake when they are completely dry.

Mince pies and biscuits

If you're making your own mince pies here are some ideas to give them a new look with alternative tops.

Instead of covering the mincemeat with shortcrust pastry lids, try making a shortcrust base, filling it with mincemeat and topping with:

- Chopped mixed nuts

- Marzipan shapes or grated marzipan

- Meringue

- Chopped apple sprinkled with lemon juice to prevent it turning brown

- A crumble topping (rub 50g/2oz butter into 100g/4oz plain flour, stir in 50g/2oz caster sugar and sprinkle the crumble mix on top of the pies)

Mince pies

Mince pies were originally oval to represent the manger in which the infant Jesus was laid. Three spices were used in the filling as a reminder of the gifts from the three kings. But originally mincemeat contained minced mutton, as well as the now familiar fruit and spices.

Mincemeat blondies

*Like a brownie without chocolate – delicious
with a glass of mulled wine*

Makes 9 to 12

175g/6oz self-raising flour

175g/6oz light soft brown sugar

50g/2oz soft margarine

1 large egg

4tbsp sweet mincemeat

1. Preheat the oven to 180°C/Gas 4. Grease the sides and line
    the base of a 20cm-square (8-inch) baking tin with baking
    parchment or greaseproof paper.

2. Put all the ingredients in a mixing bowl and beat together for
    3 minutes until well combined. Spoon the mixture into the
    prepared tins and level the top.

3. Bake for 40 minutes until the blondie is firm in the centre.

4. Cool slightly and cut into 9 or 12 pieces. Remove from the tin
    and place on a wire cooling rack. When completely cold store in
    an airtight container.

Spicy treacle buns

Delicious eaten straight from the oven with a cup of steaming hot chocolate

Makes 20

175g/6oz self-raising flour
1 level tsp baking powder
75g/3oz soft brown sugar
½ level tsp mixed spice
75g/3oz sultanas
50g/2oz black treacle
50g/2oz soft margarine
1 egg, lightly beaten

1. Preheat the oven to 200°C/Gas 6. Line 20 cake tins with paper cake cases.

2. Place the flour, baking powder, brown sugar, spice and sultanas into a mixing bowl. Gently heat the treacle and margarine in a saucepan until the margarine has melted. Allow to cool for 10 minutes. (To speed up the cooling time place the base of the saucepan in a bowl of cold water.) Make a well in the dry ingredients and pour in the treacle and margarine, along with the lightly beaten egg. Mix together thoroughly with a wooden spoon.

3. Divide the mixture between the cake cases and bake in the oven for 15 to 20 minutes until the cakes are well risen and firm to the touch. Cool for 10 minutes and serve. Or allow to become cold and store in an airtight container. They can be reheated in a warm oven, or served cold.

Ginger crisps

A crisp, mild ginger biscuit

Makes 24

175g/6oz self-raising flour

¼tsp bicarbonate of soda

1 level tsp ground ginger

75g/3oz caster sugar

75g/3oz butter or margarine

1 level tbsp golden syrup

1. Preheat the oven to 180°C/Gas 4. Line baking sheets with baking parchment.

2. Place the flour, bicarbonate of soda and ground ginger into a mixing bowl. Put the sugar, butter or margarine and syrup into a saucepan and heat gently until the butter or margarine is melted. Stir into the dry ingredients and mix to form a stiff dough.

3. Shape into 24 small balls and place on baking sheets. Allow plenty of space between each ball, as they will spread. Bake for 15 to 18 minutes until the biscuits are golden brown. Leave to cool for 10 minutes, then transfer to wire cooling racks to get cold. Store in airtight containers.

10

Party Time

Christmas seems to put us all in the mood to party – so why not slot in some entertaining? With your house beautifully decorated and your tree sparkling from top to toe, you're halfway there. Christmas entertaining doesn't have to be elaborate, expensive, or time-consuming.

Drinks parties, informal suppers and buffets are the simplest options for Christmas entertaining.

As soon as you have finalised dates and decided how many people to invite, get your invitations sent out – your guests may have busy Christmas diaries. Ask them to RSVP – not knowing how many people to expect is just one more thing to raise your stress levels!

- Plan your food and drink, and get what you can delivered

- Make lists of everything you need to buy or make

- If you plan to make some (or all) of the party food yourself, try to include some items you can make ahead and freeze

Drinks parties

Early-evening drinks parties are always popular at Christmas time. They don't need to last long – a bonus for the busy hostess, and for guests who may have plans for later in the evening.

All you need to provide is a few plates of tasty canapés and savouries, nuts and nibbles and some nice wine. A couple of plates of sweet items like mini-meringues, choux buns or little mince pies are always welcome towards the end of the party, but not essential.

If you're short of time

With just one trip to the supermarket and delicatessen you can quickly load up a trolley with hot and cold canapés, nuts, posh crisps and nibbles. All you'll have to do is warm the hot canapés in the oven, arrange the cold canapés on serving plates, and put the nibbles in bowls. How's that for quick and easy?

Another option if you're short of time is to order plates of canapés – some of the supermarkets and food stores offer party food services. All you have to do is pick them up on the day. Look for leaflets in the stores or check out their websites.

If you want to save money

The easiest way to save is to make your own canapés. Limit yourself to two or three kinds of hot canapés and three or four cold canapés. Set aside an hour or two to make the hot canapés – they could be as simple as spicy chicken pieces on cocktail sticks, cheesy puff-pastry circles, and squares of ciabatta spread with tomato purée and topped with sliced roasted red pepper and grated Parmesan.

To make the food go further make a simple dip or fresh salsa, place in the centre of a large serving plate and surround with vegetable crudités and savoury biscuits.

Serve chilled white wine or a mulled red wine. You don't need to use expensive wines when you are going to add spices and fruits to them (or you might find it cheaper to buy bottles of mulled wine, particularly if there's a special offer).

If you want to splurge

Call in the experts. Caterers will be happy to do everything for you, including arranging for waiting staff to serve the food if you want them to. If you do decide to call in the experts, make sure that you book early. Ask to see – and taste – samples before you order.

Homemade canapés

Here are some simple canapé ideas.

- Bake cocktail sausages in a medium oven (180°C/Gas 4) or fry until cooked. Drain the sausages and place in a bowl with a little grainy mustard and maple syrup and toasted sesame seeds. Dip one end of the cooked sausages in the mixture. Arrange on a serving plate.

- Place tortilla chips on a baking sheet, add a small knob of Gruyère or Cheddar and top with a slice of cherry tomato or olive. Bake in a medium oven (180°C/Gas 4) until the cheese has melted.

- Pipe soft garlic and herb cheese into ready-made cocktail-size filo pastry tartlet cases and top with a tiny twist of cucumber.

- Cut bite-sized circles from brown or white bread, brush with olive oil and pop them into a low oven to crisp. Allow to cool, then pipe on cream cheese. Add a small piece of smoked salmon and a tiny sprig of dill. Dust with black pepper.

- Top ready-made cocktail blinis with cream cheese, a small cone of salami and a basil leaf.

- Make cheesy mustard bites using a sheet of ready-rolled puff pastry. Spread with French mustard, sprinkle over finely grated Cheddar and chopped parsley. Starting with a narrow edge roll the filled pastry into a sausage and cut into 1cm-thick circles. Bake in the oven (200°C/Gas 6) for 10 to 12 minutes.

- Peel the shells from ready-cooked tiger prawns, leaving the tip of the tail on. Dip each prawn in sweet chilli sauce and then in toasted sesame seeds.

If you've time to spare

If you have the time, and enjoy cooking, making all your own canapés will certainly impress your guests.

Stuck for inspiration? You'll find whole books devoted to canapés in bookshops and in the library. There are also often features in the Christmas issues of magazines with new and innovative ideas for drinks and party food.

- Cut a ciabatta or baguette into thin slices, brush with olive oil and bake in a low oven until crisp. Cool the slices. Spread with a smooth caramelised onion chutney and top with a thin slice of flavoursome cheese and a tiny wedge of green dessert apple.

- Thread a basil leaf, a baby mozzarella ball, a wedge of fresh fig and a small roll of prosciutto, on to a cocktail stick.

- Make cocktail-sized cheese scones. Split and top with flavoured cream cheeses and a few pieces of chive, a slice of olive or a twist of cucumber.

Tips for serving canapés

- Keep your canapés small enough to be eaten in one or two bites

- Don't overload your serving plates – the canapés should be in a single layer

- Arrange hot and cold canapés on separate plates

- Have two or three kinds on each plate

- A few plates of crudités and dips, and bowls of nuts, 'posh' crisps and savoury nibbles around the room for guests to dip into will make the canapés go further

- Always drain fried hot canapés on kitchen paper before transferring to a serving plate

- As a general guide allow six to eight canapés per person for a two-hour party and eight to ten if the party is planned to last longer

Drinks

Limit your drinks to red and white wine and a selection of non-alcoholic drinks. Guests don't expect to be offered spirits. As it's Christmas you might like to serve a warming mulled wine or a fruit punch.

Get a friend or partner to make sure that glasses are replenished, so you can concentrate on the food.

How much drink?

- Allow two bottles of white wine to each bottle of red.

- As a guide, allow two and a half glasses of wine for a two-hour drinks party, and one soft drink per person.

- Allow two to three glasses of soft drinks for guests not drinking alcohol.

- A 750ml (25fl.oz) bottle of wine will serve five glasses and from a 750ml bottle of champagne expect to get six glasses.

- Try to buy your wines on 'sale or return' so you can order a little extra and return any unopened bottles. To save money settle on one white and one red wine, so you can take advantages of special offers on multiple orders of the same wine.

Anthea's Top Tip

Enlist the help of friends or older children to help you hand around the canapés. If you are short of help arrange the food on tables around the room – it also encourages the guests to mingle. Remember to have plenty of napkins for sticky fingers and coasters to protect your furniture.

Dips

Quick dips to serve with crudités, crisps and savoury biscuits.

Curry and honey dip

Serves 10

150ml/10fl.oz soured cream

225g/8oz jar good-quality mayonnaise

2tbsp medium curry paste

1tbsp runny honey

Combine the soured cream and mayonnaise in a bowl. Add the curry powder and the honey and mix together.

Cucumber dip

Serves 12

150ml/10fl.oz soured cream

225g/8oz jar good-quality mayonnaise

1 cucumber, peeled

1tsp mixed herbs

Freshly ground black pepper

Combine the soured cream and mayonnaise in a bowl. Remove the seeds from the cucumber. Grate the cucumber. Place the grated cucumber on a pad of kitchen towel and squeeze out any excess water. Add to the cream and mayonnaise mix, with the mixed herbs. Season with black pepper.

Christmas carol evening

If you're attending a carol concert or singing carols round a Christmas tree, why not end the evening by inviting friends and family back for a party?

Turn on the Christmas tree lights, serve some simple refreshments and greet guests with a warming drink – both alcoholic and non-alcoholic – and you have the recipe for an enjoyable evening.

You could serve a selection of nuts, crisps, tortilla chips and dips, and savouries. For something sweet offer mince pies, or hand-made truffles.

If you want to serve something more substantial give your guests bowls of steaming homemade soup with warm crispy rolls followed by slices of a luxury mince pie and cream. Or 'glam up' your favourite chilli recipe and serve with a bowl of fluffy rice.

If you are short of time, you can buy everything you need from the supermarket or deli. Or if you are trying to keep your budget down, you could ask friends to bring something to add to a buffet table. But do give them some idea of the kind of buffet you have in mind.

Anthea's Top Tip

Try this mince pie magic. Cheat a little by buying luxury mince pies and warming them in the oven. Then lift the tops and drop in a teaspoon of brandy butter. Replace the tops and sprinkle with icing sugar. Arrange on a plate with a sprig of holly. Delicious!

Party drinks

Get into the festive spirit with these seasonal concoctions.

Mulled wine

Turn the clock back with this eighteenth-century recipe

Makes 8 to 10 glasses

1 bottle red wine

12 sugar lumps

6 cloves

600ml/20fl.oz boiling water

½ small wine glass brandy

1 small wine glass orange curaçao

Grated nutmeg

Oranges and apples, cubed, to serve

Place the sugar, cloves and wine in a large saucepan and heat until it almost reaches boiling point. Add the curaçao, brandy and boiling water. Immediately pour into heatproof glasses and grate a little nutmeg on top. Add pieces of cubed orange and apple to serve.

Mulled claret and port

A warming favourite on a cold night

Makes 8 glasses

1 bottle of claret

½ bottle ruby port

1 stick of cinnamon, broken in two

Thinly pared rind of a lemon

6 cloves

100g/4oz soft light brown sugar

Place all of the ingredients into a large saucepan and heat gently until the liquid is almost boiling. Simmer very gently for 5 minutes. Strain through a fine sieve and serve immediately with a crisp cinnamon biscuit.

Driver's punch

A delicious non-alcoholic punch

Serves 12 to 15

1.2 litres/2 pints apple juice

1.2 litres/2 pints orange juice

Ginger ale

Orange and apple slices

A lime or orange studded with 6 cloves

Combine the apple juice and orange juice in a large glass jug, then top up with ginger ale (if it is a little too sweet add a dash of soda water). Add the orange and apple slices and the lime or orange studded with cloves. Serve at room temperature or over ice cubes made with orange or apple juice.

Hot cider punch

A warming fruity punch

Makes 10 to 12 glasses

3 small eating apples

6 cloves

1 litre/40fl.oz still cider

50g/2oz light soft brown sugar

1 stick cinnamon

1tsp ground ginger

150ml/5fl.oz water

2 small oranges, sliced into circles

1. Remove the cores from the centre of the apples and score round the centre of each apple. Stud each of the apples with 2 cloves. Place the apples on a baking sheet and bake in the oven (180°C/ Gas 4) for 20 minutes.

2. Place the cider in a saucepan and heat gently. Do not boil.

3. In a small saucepan place the water, cinnamon stick, ground ginger and sugar. Heat, stirring, until the sugar has dissolved, then simmer gently for 5 minutes. Sieve into a small bowl.

4. Place the baked apples and the orange slices into a large heatproof bowl, add the sieved sugar water and the warmed cider, and serve.

Informal buffet suppers

An informal buffet supper is the perfect solution when you want to entertain a large group at Christmas.

It's a good idea to have the event as far ahead of Christmas Day as you can. Keep the food simple – with the sumptuous Christmas setting and scintillating conversation your guests really won't notice. But try to give the food a festive feel by introducing something Christmassy – even if it's only tiny ginger biscuits or Christmas pudding truffles (bought or homemade) served at the end of the meal.

When you are planning the menu try to include some dishes that can be frozen ahead, bought ready-made, or served cold and only need 'construction'. The same goes for accompaniments. Don't be tempted to do too many dishes.

If you are pressed for time no one will mind if you decide to raid the supermarket or deli for some ready-made dishes. But if you can find time to make some of the dishes on your menu, it's much more fun.

As always when you are cheating a little (or a lot), do it with style. Garnish the dishes beautifully. If, for example, you buy a classic meat-cooked-in-wine casserole, bake some small circles of puff pastry brushed with egg yolk and arrange them in an overlapping circle on top of the casserole, and sprinkle on some chopped fresh parsley to give it a home-cooked feel. Or make some tiny savoury scones to transfer a simple casserole into a cobbler.

If you buy a chilled or frozen dessert, choose ones that can be easily transferred to smart serving dishes and then 'personalised' with your own decoration – it need only be a few mint leaves, some fresh fruit or a dusting of snowy icing sugar.

A main course and a dessert are all you need. But you could serve a plate or two of canapés with drinks before supper or end the meal with a cheese board.

In the drinks department, some red and white wine and a variety of soft drinks will be all you need.

How much food?

If you are entertaining fewer than twenty people, then two or at most three main dishes are plenty. Generally a choice of a hot and a cold dish or just cold dishes, along with accompaniments such as rice, pasta or potatoes, and appropriate vegetables or salads are all you will need.

Tips for a successful buffet

- Choose dishes that can be eaten with just a fork.

- Slice cold cooked meats thinly so they can be cut with the side of the fork.

- Include a dish suitable for vegetarians or vegans.

- Serve trifles or 'soft' desserts in individual dishes, as large dishes of trifle can quickly look messy. Or opt for tortes, cheesecakes and tarts, which can be cut into slices in advance and served with cream or crème fraîche.

- If possible have a couple of tables available for elderly guests and children who may find it difficult to eat with their plates on their laps.

Wine

Chill white wine in the fridge for two hours before serving. If your fridge is filled with party food put the bottles in large plastic buckets with ice for an hour. (If you might want to return some of the unused bottles to the wine merchants, slip the bottles into sturdy freezer bags to prevent the labels floating off.)

Most red wines are served at room temperature. Check the label or ask your wine merchant for advice.

Sparkling wine and champagne should be kept in the fridge until they are needed. The colder they are the more bubbles they will have!

The buffet table

Make your buffet table a feast for the eyes. Cover it with a crisp white tablecloth and place a festive arrangement in the centre.

To help prevent bottlenecks as your guests are serving themselves try to position it so it can be reached from three sides.

Arrange your table in a logical fashion so guests can pick up a plate first and then proceed to walk down the table making their selections. The hot dishes and their accompaniments, if you are serving any, should be reached first, followed by the cold dishes. Finish with a basket of interesting bread or rolls and butters. Condiments, pickles and sauces are usually placed at the end of the table, just before the cutlery and napkins. Remember to place serving spoons and forks by the dishes.

When the first course is finished, clear the table and remove any debris (if the tablecloth has got horribly messy, it's a good idea to have a second small white cloth handy to drop over). Allow a short time to elapse before you lay out the desserts along with dessert plates, bowls and cutlery.

If you are serving coffee and chocolates after the buffet have everything on trays in the kitchen so that it's ready to bring in when needed.

Anthea's Top Tips

If you are short of wine-chilling space don't forget 'nature's fridge' – just pop the bottles outside the back door to get cold.

Have a drinks table away from the buffet if you can – it will cut down congestion and the danger of spilled drinks.

A festive supper

Entertain your friends to supper with ease and style. Try this ten-minute starter, freeze-ahead main course and a cold ready-made light dessert. What could be easier?

A Festive Supper for Six

Spicy prawns in lettuce

Herby cranberry lamb in red wine

or

Your favourite 'never fail' casserole

with

Creamy mashed potatoes

Broccoli and green beans

A lemon or chocolate torte topped with a mound of
fresh raspberries and dusted with icing sugar

Spicy prawns in lettuce

Serves 6

2tbsp oil

1 small onion, finely chopped

2 cloves garlic, crushed

1 small red pepper, deseeded and finely chopped

½ inch fresh ginger, finely grated

Salt

1tbsp mild curry paste

2tbsp white vinegar

500g/18oz small frozen prawns, defrosted

55ml/2fl.oz fresh double cream

1 small red chilli, deseeded and finely chopped

8 small iceberg lettuce leaves

A few sprigs of flat-leaf parsley or coriander leaves

1. Add the oil to a large nonstick frying pan and gently fry the onion, garlic, red pepper, chilli and ginger until it is soft. Add a pinch of salt and the curry paste and fry for a minute.

2. Add the vinegar, sugar and prawns and heat through. Don't overcook the prawns or they will be tough. Stir in the cream and warm, but don't allow to boil.

3. Place the lettuce leaves on 6 small serving plates and spoon the prawn mixture into the leaves. Add a sprig of parsley or coriander and serve immediately.

4. To save time prepare the recipe until the stage at which the prawns are added. Set aside. It will only take you a couple of minutes to add the prawns and warm them through, while your guests are relaxing with a drink.

Herby cranberry lamb in red wine

Serves 6

2tbsp olive oil

1kg lean leg of lamb, bone removed, and cut into large cubes

12 baby onions or one large union cut into wedges

4 carrots, peeled and thickly sliced

3 small leeks, cut into chunks

1 clove garlic, crushed

4 sprigs of rosemary

2 bay leaves

1 bottle red wine

2tbsp cranberry jelly (or redcurrant jelly)

150ml/5fl.oz lamb stock (made with a cube)

Salt and freshly ground black pepper

20g/¾oz butter, made into a paste with 1tbsp plain flour

1. Pour the oil into a large heavy based saucepan and fry the lamb until it is brown on all sides. Remove from the pan and set aside.

2. Add the onions to the pan and cook for 10 minutes before adding the carrots, leeks and garlic. Fry for a further 5 minutes.

3. Return the meat to the pan and add the rosemary, bay leaves, red wine, cranberry jelly, and sufficient stock to cover the meat and vegetables. Season with salt and pepper. Bring to the boil, reduce the heat, cover the pan and simmer very gently for 1 to 1¼ hours or until the meat is tender.

4. Remove the bay leaves and the sprigs of rosemary and discard. Using a slotted spoon remove the meat and vegetables and place in a casserole dish. Whisk the butter and flour paste into the sauce remaining in the pan, a little at a time, and cook over a low heat until it thickens. Pour the sauce over the meat and vegetables.

5. Serve immediately or cool quickly and place in the fridge to use the following day or freeze.

To freeze: Cool the dish in the fridge. When completely cold place the dish and its contents in the freezer. As soon as it is frozen remove the contents, place in a large freezer bag. When you are ready to serve the casserole, remove the bag from the freezer, put the contents back in the original casserole dish and defrost in the fridge overnight. Reheat in the oven until piping hot. Serve with creamy mashed potatoes and green vegetables.

If you want to save money

If you are making a large casserole and want to cut the cost:

- Reduce the quantity of meat and add a tin or two of canned mixed beans to meat casseroles, or white beans (soya or cannellini) to chicken casseroles. Simply drain and rinse the beans and add to the casserole for the last ten minutes of cooking time. (If you plan to freeze the dish add the beans when you reheat it.)

- Substitute chicken thighs for chicken breast. Thighs are very tasty but need a longer cooking time, particularly if you are not removing the bones. Skim off any excess fat at the end of the cooking time.

Berry delicious dessert

Serves 6

1kg/2¼lb frozen red berry fruits, defrosted
2–4tbsp icing sugar
Ready-made meringue stars
2tbsp brandy (optional)
A large tub of double cream, lightly whipped

1. Place the berry fruits in a large bowl. Add the icing sugar and stir gently.
2. In a second bowl arrange the meringue stars.
3. Lightly whip the cream and fold in the brandy, if used.

Let guests help themselves to this gloriously simple dessert.

Christmas baked apples

Serves 6

6 small cooking or large tart eating apples
1 jar luxury mincemeat
6tbsp water
Honey
Slivered almonds to decorate

1. With the tip of a knife, cut round the centre of each apple, so that it does not split while baking. Remove the core and fill with mincemeat. Place the apples in an ovenproof dish. Add the water to the dish and drizzle the apples with honey or golden syrup.
2. Bake for 30 to 40 minutes in a 180°C/Gas 4 oven until the apples are soft but not collapsed. Transfer to serving plates and pour over any liquid in the dish. Scatter over the almonds. Serve with whipped cream or crème fraîche.

Mum's quick trifle

Serves 6–8

1 tin of raspberries, drained

1 tin chopped mixed fruit, drained

1 jam-filled Swiss roll

3tbsp sherry

500ml/18fl.oz carton luxury ready-made custard

300g/11oz double cream, lightly whipped

2 Flake bars, lightly crumbled

1. Slice the Swiss roll into eight slices and place in the bottom of a glass serving bowl. Sprinkle over the sherry, raspberries and mixed fruit.

2. Spoon over the custard and top with a layer of cream. Chill in the fridge. Decorate with the crumbled Flake bars just before serving.

Coffee and pear trifle

Serves 6

6 individual frozen chocolate mousses

1 Madeira or coffee sponge cake

A miniature of coffee liqueur (Tia Maria or Kahlua)

1 large tin pears, drained and chopped

150g/6oz chocolate-covered digestive biscuits, crushed

2tsp instant coffee dissolved in 1tbsp boiling water

1 large carton luxury custard

300g/10fl.oz double cream, lightly whipped

To decorate

Chocolate-covered coffee beans and fresh mint leaves

1. Defrost the chocolate mousses. Cut the cake into small squares and place in the base of six small dishes or glasses. Drizzle over the liqueur. Add the chopped pears to each of the glasses. Spoon the chocolate mousse over and level the tops.

2. Sprinkle over the crushed digestive biscuits. Dissolve the instant coffee in a tablespoon of boiling water and allow to become cold. Stir the coffee into the custard and spoon the coffee/custard mix over the biscuit layer. Lightly whip the cream and spoon over the custard.

3. Chill for 2 hours. Just before serving decorate with chocolate-covered coffee beans and mint leaves.

Toffee apple tipsy pudding

Comfort food at its best

Serves 8

50g/2oz butter

6 medium tart eating apples, peeled, cored and cut into wedges

175g/6oz caster sugar

570ml/1 pint double cream

400g/14oz brioche loaf cut into 2cm/¾-inch slices, and then each slice cut diagonally into 2 triangles

3tbsp brandy (optional)

75g/3oz sultanas

4 medium egg yolks

Yogurt or crème fraîche to serve

1. Preheat the oven to 180°C/Gas 4.

2. Melt the butter in a frying pan but do not allow to burn. Add the apples and 150g of the sugar and cook over a moderate heat for 5 minutes until the sugar and butter have caramelised and the apples have begun to soften. Stir in the cream, bring the pan back to the boil and simmer gently for a minute. Strain the apples over a bowl to reserve the creamy sauce to use later.

3. Place a layer of the brioche slices on the bottom of a lightly buttered ovenproof pie dish. Place the apples over the brioche layer. Sprinkle with the brandy, if used, and the sultanas. Arrange the remaining brioche triangles so they are overlapping on the top. Whisk the egg yolks into the reserved cream and pour over the brioche. Sprinkle with the remaining sugar.

4. Bake in the oven for 35 to 40 minutes until golden and crisp. Serve with yogurt or crème fraîche.

If you want to save money

It's not what you serve but the way you serve it. Pay attention to the presentation and, whatever you serve, give it a touch of class.

A fabulous cheese board, accompanied by fruit, chutneys, pickles and a selection of interesting breads and crackers can make a sumptuous supper for a crowd, without breaking the bank.

To complete the feast give a Christmas twist to an ever-popular but inexpensive dessert – such as an apple crumble layered with brandy-soaked mincemeat and a crunchy nutty crumble topping – and you're there.

If you want something more exotic try a mango, pear and chocolate crumble. Or perhaps serve honey-drizzled Christmas baked apples filled with mincemeat and served with whipped cream (they can be made in advance, cooked and reheated).

If you want to splurge

Find a reliable cook or a caterer to prepare a selection of buffet or supper dishes and desserts for you.

Say Cheese!

If you are serving a cheese supper or a cheese board to end the perfect meal, resist the temptation to buy a wide selection of small pieces of cheese – they will quickly dry out and soon resemble something more suitable for a mousetrap than a cheese board. Instead opt for larger pieces of three or four cheeses with different textures and flavours that you enjoy. (If you are feeling adventurous and would like to try something new, always ask to taste before you buy.)

Here are four different kinds of cheeses, which would make a perfect cheese board:

- A tasty mature Cheddar

- A mellow Leicester

- A soft or semi-soft cheese such as Camembert, Brie or Saint-Nectaire

- A blue cheese, like Stilton or Gorgonzola, or a goats' cheese

What to serve with cheese

For an after-dinner cheese board choose crispy biscuits, crackers or oatcakes. Avoid biscuits that are highly salted or heavily flavoured, as they will mask the flavour of the cheese. If you are serving cheese as part of a supper buffet also include baskets of freshly baked bread or small rolls. Don't forget some really nice butter and perhaps an olive spread.

You can also serve grapes, fresh dates, quartered fresh figs, apples and pears or kiwi fruit with your cheese board.

Allow the flavours of cheese to develop by removing them from the fridge an hour before serving.

Guests to stay

Having guests to stay is all part of the Christmas fun – but there's no denying it can sometimes be quite a challenge trying to find somewhere for everyone to sleep. But be relaxed about it – your guests are coming to spend time with you, they won't be expecting you to provide five-star luxury.

Younger guests will be quite happy with a sofa bed or a blow-up mattress in the lounge but older guests will really appreciate a proper bed and a little privacy.

Where children are concerned it's generally a case of 'the more the merrier' and your children will probably be only too happy to make room for visiting youngsters – but don't expect a quiet time, particularly on Christmas Eve!

If you have a guest room prepare it well in advance and then you can close the door and forget about it until the day your guests arrive.

Remember that it's the personal touches that make all the difference.

- Make a space in the wardrobe and clear a couple of drawers so they can unpack their clothes. Have some empty coat hangers ready.

- When you make the bed up include a couple of extra pillows and drape a warm throw over the end of the bed in case they are chilly during the night.

First-time guests

Send them a map or clear instructions and your telephone number in case they get lost.

When your guests arrive take them on a quick tour of the house and then take them to their room so they can unpack and relax, particularly if they have had a long journey.

If they are staying for more than a few days show them where the washing machine is and where you keep the iron and ironing board.

Remember to give your guests some quiet time that they can spend on their own.

- Lay out bath towels, hand towels and flannels. Put a non-slip rubber mat in the bath or shower, particularly if your guests are elderly or children.

- Set out a basket of small-sized toiletries and a comb.

- Put an alarm clock on the bedside table, just in case your guests forget to bring one.

On the day they arrive put fresh flowers in the room, and check the temperature.

It is also a nice gesture to provide them with a 'hospitality' tray – a small jar of coffee, tea, individual cartons of milk, sugar, a small tin of biscuits, cups, saucers, tea spoons and a kettle – in case they are early risers and desperate for a cup of tea before you are up and about. Don't forget some water and glasses.

When your guests leave give them a 'travel survival kit' for the journey – snacks, a bottle of water, cartons of fruit juice, a tube of mints or boiled sweets and a packet of wet wipes.

11

Christmas Day

It's Christmas Day. With the weeks of planning, preparation and present-buying behind you, all that's left to do now is cook the Christmas lunch. So take a deep breath, make yourself a time plan so you know when everything needs to be done, rope in some help and have fun.

Place settings

Take a large fir cone, bought from a florist or found in a wood. Rub the bottom with sandpaper to give it a flat surface and attach to the table with Blu Tak. Leave as it is or spray to match your colour scheme, and attach your guests' name tags. Alternatively, you can use Christmas crackers (see page 81).

The Christmas bird

William Strickland introduced turkeys into England in 1526 after buying six of the birds from a Native American trader. Until that time the most popular festive fare among the wealthy was swan, peacock and pheasant.

The Christmas table – setting the scene

Simple and stylish is the look to aim for when you're laying your Christmas table. You don't need to spend money on glass beads, sequined stars, or silk rose petals to turn your table into a work of art.

Keep your table settings simple. Resist the temptation to include glasses and cutlery that won't be used during the meal.

Cover your table with a crisp white tablecloth, add white napkins, a simple table decoration, and use whatever china and glassware you have.

Decorating your napkins

- Tie a piece of narrow velvet ribbon round a folded napkin and slip a small Christmas rose underneath.

- Tie a white linen napkin around three breadsticks and tuck in a sprig of fresh rosemary or a small sprig of holly (preferably a non-prickly variety).

- Plait raffia and tie around a napkin; add a few bay leaves or a sprig of holly.

- Rummage through the remnant box at your local fabric shop for unusual trimmings like lace, pearls or tiny tassels to make napkin rings.

Table decorations

Keep table decorations simple:

- **Fill a low vase with red roses and white feathers.**

- **Use a ring of oasis, some festive foliage and a candle to make an elegant centre piece.**

Christmas breakfast

Try one of these quick Christmas morning breakfasts to keep everyone going until lunch time:

- Buy some Scotch pancakes – you'll need three or four for a serving. Warm the pancakes in the oven. Grill some lean back bacon until crisp. Place a stack of pancakes on a plate, top with the bacon and drizzle with maple syrup.

- Toast two small bought waffles. Place one of the toasted waffles on a plate, top with fresh raspberries, then dust with icing sugar. Top with the second waffle. Scatter a few more raspberries on the top and dust with icing sugar again. Serve with yogurt or fromage frais.

- Split and toast a wholemeal English muffin. Top with creamy scrambled egg with smoked salmon.

Anthea's Top Tip

If you don't want your little ones snacking on sweets on Christmas Day keep bowls of ready-prepared fruit – mandarins, satsumas, apple slices, figs, dates, ready-to-eat dried apricots cut into slices, ready-to-eat dried banana – handy for them to dip into. (I know it's the right thing to do but I'm afraid that in my house this idea would be about as popular as a blockage in the vacuum cleaner!)

Festive sparkle

Put some fizz into your celebrations by serving one of these easy champagne cocktails before lunch:

- *Bucks Fizz* – Half fizz and half orange juice
- *Bellini* – A glass of fizz topped up with peach juice
- *Kir Royale* – A glass of fizz topped with a dash of cassis

Fizz rules

- Open champagne by covering the cork with a clean cloth and holding it firmly. Then turn the bottle while holding the cork still.

- Champagne will not spray across the room if you chill it well for several hours before opening.

- Wash champagne flutes in clear hot water and allow to air dry. A trace of washing-up liquid will kill bubbles in seconds.

First-time nerves

If this is your first full-scale Christmas dinner – or if you are short of time – here are some tips to help you keep your cool:

- Keep your menu REALLY simple.

- Lay the table the evening before and get out all the serving dishes you will need. Also lay out a tray with cups and saucers, sugar bowl and cream jug for coffee. (Slip sticky notes on the dishes so you can remember what's going in them. They'll be a great help if anyone lends a hand in the kitchen.)

- Skip the starter – you really won't need one.

- Get all the vegetables peeled, prepared and ready to cook the day before.

- Limit vegetable accompaniments to two dishes – no one will go hungry.

- Buy the accompaniments for your turkey – the cranberry sauce, bread sauce, stuffing, and even the gravy.

- No one will know you haven't cooked it from scratch, so buy your Christmas pudding – and the sauces to go with it.

- If carving the turkey at the table fills you with dread get someone else to do it. Carve it in the kitchen and arrange it on a large platter, or better still buy a boned turkey joint or crown.

- Enlist all the help you can muster.

Christmas Lunch

With all the preparations done, and your time plan by your side, cooking the Christmas lunch should be a breeze. Remember it's only a Sunday lunch with a cracker.

Christmas Lunch

Blinis with cream cheese, smoked salmon and caviar

Golden roast turkey with pigs in blankets, stuffing balls, cranberry sauce and bread sauce

Roast potatoes

Roasted roots

Brussels sprouts

Christmas pudding with St Clement's whisky sauce and cream

The Starter

There really is no need for a starter but if you do want to serve one choose something cold and simple like some light and delicious smoked salmon blinis. Simply make a plate or two of them, open a bottle of bubbly or make a champagne cocktail and let your guests help themselves while you put the finishing touches to the Christmas feast.

Smoked salmon blinis

Serves 8

2 packets ready-to-serve blinis

250g/9oz cream cheese

350g/12oz thinly sliced smoked salmon

Caviar or lumpfish roe

Spread the blinis with a little cream cheese and top with smoked salmon and the tip of a teaspoon of caviar or lumpfish roe. Arrange on a platter.

The main course

Preparing and roasting a turkey:

Remember to take the turkey out of the fridge an hour before you want to start cooking it, to allow it to come up to room temperature.

1. Stuff the neck of the turkey with your stuffing then smooth the flap of skin over the stuffing, tucking it under the bird (you can insert a halved lemon and onion into the body cavity for extra flavour, if you like).

2. Place the turkey into a roasting tin (or on a trivet in a roasting tin). Cover the breast with streaky bacon. Brush the bird with melted butter.

3. Cover loosely with foil, shiny side down.

4. Roast the turkey for the calculated time. Remove the foil for the last 45 minutes of the cooking time to allow the skin to become golden.

5. Check that the turkey is cooked by inserting a skewer into the thickest part of the thigh. The juices should run clear. If they are not clear return the turkey to the oven for another 20 minutes before testing again.

6. When it is cooked remove the turkey from the roasting tin on to a large platter. Cover with foil and a clean tea towel. Allow the turkey to rest for 20 to 45 minutes, depending on its size, before you carve it. Not only will it allow the meat to relax but it will also free up the oven and give you time to turn up the dial if anything else in the oven needs an extra burst of heat.

7. Arrange pigs in blankets, stuffing balls etc. around the bird. Tuck a bunch of parsley and sage at the back of the bird.

If your turkey weighs 5kg it's easy to work out how long to cook it. But what if it weighs 5.65kg? Not so easy! Don't guess or panic. Just go to www.britishturkey.co.uk where you'll find a roasting calculator to do the maths for you. There are also plenty of other helpful tips on the website.

Roasting times

Roast turkeys at 190°C/Gas 5 (170°C/Gas 3 if you have a fan-assisted oven).

For turkeys weighing over 4kg roast for 20 minutes per kilo plus 90 minutes.

For smaller birds and turkey joints weighing less than 4kg roast for 20 minutes per kilo plus 70 minutes.

Remember to weigh your turkey after it has been stuffed when you are calculating the roasting time needed.

Carving a turkey

If you want to carve clean, succulent-looking slices from your turkey, make sure your carving knife is very sharp. When you are serving turkey, serve each person with both white meat from the breast and dark meat from the legs.

Turkey talk

What size turkey will I need?

2.25kg/5lb	serves 2 to 4
3.6kg/8lb	serves 6 to 8
5.6kg/12lb	serves 10 to 12
9kg/20lb	serves 12 to 15

Frozen turkeys:

- If you buy a frozen turkey remember to check on the packaging well in advance, to see how long it will take to defrost. You don't want to look on Christmas Eve and discover it needs forty-eight hours!

- Defrost the turkey slowly in the bottom of the fridge. Don't let it touch or drip on other foods. Aim to have it completely thawed by the evening of Christmas Eve.

- If the turkey goes into the oven before it is completely defrosted it's likely that the core temperature will not get high enough, which means there is a risk of food poisoning. Check whether the giblets are inside the turkey and remove them, as they could be in a plastic bag.

- Wipe the inside and outside of the turkey with kitchen paper.

Stuffing a turkey

It isn't recommended that you stuff the cavity of the turkey. This is because the temperature in the middle of the stuffing may not reach a high enough temperature for a sufficient amount of time to kill any bacteria present.

If you do put stuffing in the neck of the turkey, never do this until just before you are ready to roast it. This will reduce the risk of contamination from bacteria.

Pigs in blankets

Pork cocktail sausages wrapped in thin crispy bacon are a traditional accompaniment to turkey

Serves 8

1 packet thin-cut streaky bacon (or pancetta)

A little Dijon mustard

1 packet good-quality pork cocktail sausages

1. Place the bacon on a board and stretch each rasher by running along them with the flat of a knife. Spread a little mustard on the rashers. Cut into two or three pieces.

2. Wrap a piece of bacon or pancetta around each sausage. Place on a baking tray and bake in a moderate oven (180°C/Gas 4) until the sausages are cooked and the bacon is crisp. Drain on a piece of kitchen towel and keep warm.

These can be made the day before and kept in the fridge to be reheated on Christmas Day.

Cranberry sauce

Add some zing to bought cranberry sauce by stirring in a tablespoon of fine-shred marmalade, two tablespoons of port and the finely grated zest of half an orange.

A classic gravy

1. Pour the juices and fat from the roasting tin into a jug and allow to stand for 10 minutes to separate. Skim off the fat and reserve the juices.

2. Place the roasting tin on the stove and add 2 to 3 table-spoons plain flour. Whisk well to loosen any sediment in the tin and cook for 2 to 3 minutes. Add a splash of red wine, sherry or Madeira if liked.

3. Return the juices to the tin with 600ml/1 pint chicken stock. Whisk well and bring to the boil. Simmer until slightly thickened. Taste and season with salt and pepper if necessary. Pour through a sieve if you need to remove any lumps.

This amount of gravy should serve 6 to 8 people. Always make more than you think you'll need.

Roast Potatoes

For roast potatoes that are crisp and golden on the outside and fluffy on the inside try this simple method.

Peel the potatoes and boil for 3 to 5 minutes (depending on the size of the potatoes) in lightly salted water. Drain and shake the potatoes in the pan to roughen the outsides. Sprinkle over a little flour. Transfer the potatoes to a baking tray containing some piping-hot goose fat and bake in a preheated oven (200C/Gas 6) for 40 to 45 minutes. Gently turn the potatoes a couple of times during the cooking time so they brown evenly.

If you want to add extra flavour to your roast potatoes add a few cloves of garlic – there's no need to peel them – or a whole bulb of garlic cut in half, and some sprigs of fresh thyme to the baking tray. Or add a little mustard powder to the flour before sprinkling it on the drained parboiled potatoes.

The secret of perfect roast potatoes is to use the right varieties – try Maris Piper, King Edward, Wilja, Desiree, Romana or Cara.

Anthea's Top Tip
Making gravy is prime cheating territory. You can buy really good gravy now. So, why not? You can use it as it comes or spark it up by adding the juices from your turkey or a splash of wine.

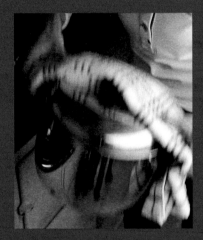

Anthea's Top Tip
You can even cook the roast potatoes the night before. When they are cooked let them cool completely before covering the tray with a piece of foil. All you have to do next day is remove the foil, put them into the oven for twenty minutes while the turkey is resting and you'll have delicious crispy roast potatoes.

Vegetables

Keep your vegetable accompaniments simple. Two or three dishes will be enough.

Brighten up your Brussels

Serve steamed or boiled Brussels sprouts simply drizzled with a little melted butter or try one of these toppings to add flavour and crunch. Do not overcook sprouts or they will be soggy.

- Dry-fry some chopped streaky bacon until crisp, add some chopped cooked chestnuts (to save time use vacuum-packed nuts) and 2 cloves of finely chopped garlic and continue frying for 2 minutes. Pour over the sprouts just before serving.

- Combine 50g/2oz of toasted flaked almonds with 50g/2oz of melted butter and spoon over the cooked sprouts.

Roasted roots

Serves 4 to 6

12 carrots (the thickness of your thumb)	6 cloves of garlic
4 parsnips	A few sprigs of fresh thyme and rosemary
3 turnips	2 bay leaves
A small swede	Olive oil
2 red onions, cut into wedges	

1. Peel the root vegetables and cut into thick batons. Peel the onions and cut into wedges. Place all of the vegetables in a saucepan of cold, lightly salted water.

2. Bring to the boil and simmer for 3 to 5 minutes. Drain the vegetables and transfer to a baking tray, add the peeled garlic cloves, the sprigs of thyme, rosemary and bay leaves. Drizzle a little olive oil over the vegetables. Shake to coat with the oil.

3. Transfer to a nonstick baking tray and bake in a moderate oven until they are cooked and golden. Transfer to a serving dish and keep warm.

Christmas pudding

Christmas pudding is the traditional finale to the festive feast but you may want to serve something lighter, such as a favourite trifle, or a dessert from the freezer.

If you opt to buy a Christmas pudding follow the reheating instructions on the packaging or use the traditional method. This means covering the basin with greaseproof paper and a pudding cloth tied with string and steaming for 1 to 1½ hours depending on the size of the pudding.

Turn the pudding out on to a deep serving plate. (Now's the time to poke silver coins or silver Christmas charms into the pudding, if you want to – but remember to warn your guests that they are there!)

To flame a Christmas pudding: Warm a little brandy – or vodka – in a saucepan, pour over the pudding and light it.

Ring the changes

Ready for a change from the traditional turkey or goose?

There are several other birds available at Christmas so why not try one of these interesting alternatives. Check your recipe books and on the Internet for festive recipes.

You will find these birds in most supermarkets and game butchers in the weeks before Christmas, either frozen or fresh.

Pheasant

A good choice if you like rich-tasting meat. They are available fresh and frozen in the weeks leading up to Christmas and will serve two or three people.

Duck

Although duck breasts are becoming more popular for meals all the year round, a whole duck still makes a special treat. Young birds weighing up to 1.8kg (4lb) and larger birds weighing as much as 3kg (6½lb) are usually available at Christmas. A small duck will feed three people and a large duck will feed five people – although there will probably only be enough left over to make a few sandwiches.

Guinea fowl

Guinea fowl are now farmed like chickens and their tender white flesh and only slightly gamey taste make them a good Christmas Day roast. But they are small, weighing between 900g (2lb) and 1.5kg (3½lb), so for four people you would need to buy two birds.

Make it a roast

A beautifully roasted succulent joint of meat makes a perfect festive feast.

It's an opportunity to buy a larger joint than you would at any other time of the year and to be imaginative with bastes and glazes (See Chapter 12).

Golden roast guinea fowl with a citrus and thyme stuffing, bacon rolls, creamy spring onion mash and traditional Christmas vegetables

If there's just the two of you, treat yourselves to something special instead of the traditional turkey, such as guinea fowl with a citrus and thyme stuffing and creamy mash (or roasties if you prefer!)

Serves 2

1 guinea fowl

4 sprigs fresh thyme

30g/1¼oz butter

1 medium egg, lightly beaten

75g/3oz fresh white breadcrumbs

Salt and freshly ground black pepper

For the stuffing

1 small onion, skinned and finely chopped

40g/1½oz butter

1 level tbsp grated lemon jest

2tbsp fresh chopped thyme

Freshly ground black pepper

For the spring onion mash

350g/12oz old potatoes

25g/1oz butter

1tbsp cream

3 spring onions, thinly sliced

Freshly ground black pepper

1. To make the stuffing: Fry the onion in 40g of butter. Place into a small mixing bowl. Add the remaining ingredients and mix together. Season with salt and pepper. Allow to cool completely. Stuff the neck cavity with the stuffing.

2. Preheat the oven to 190°C/Gas 5.

3. To prepare the guinea fowl: loosen the skin over the breast with your fingers. Spread the butter and the sprigs of thyme under the skin.

4. Roast for 1 to 1½ hours until the juices run clear.

5. To make the spring onion mash: Boil, drain and mash the potatoes, with the butter and cream. Fry the chopped spring onions in a teaspoon of oil for 2 minutes. Stir into the mashed potato. Season with pepper.

12

Boxing Day... and Beyond

Boxing Day

This is a day for relaxing so keep everything simple. If it's just the family, have a fridge raid and feast on leftovers, salads, jacket potatoes and lots of lovely pickles. (Or why not take yourself off for a day in the country and a relaxing pub lunch? The leftovers can wait for another day!)

But if you've got plenty of mouths to feed on Boxing Day – or are expecting an influx of guests – still keep it simple. Serve up a stunning cold buffet lunch, with salad vegetables and lots of pickles and fresh bread. Try to rope in as much help as you can getting everything ready. End the meal with a simple dessert – preferably one that you've made ahead and popped in the freezer, or a delicious sweet confection you picked up at the supermarket.

When you are feeding a crowd, a gammon, a ham, or a joint of beef or pork beautifully glazed makes the perfect centrepiece for a buffet table. An alternative is to serve a whole salmon.

If you do want a starter, choose something quick and tasty that everyone can share, like a selection of tapas. One trip to the deli or supermarket and you can stock up with all you need. Or as an alternative to a starter offer a cheese board at the end of the meal.

If you want to splurge

Why not gather up the girls and head for the sales? Leave the boys at home to raid the fridge for lunch.

Sumptuous sauces and gorgeous glazes

Impress your guests by turning a plain roast joint into a fabulous centrepiece for your buffet by adding a glaze.

Just combine the ingredients and brush or pour over the meat fifteen minutes before the end of the cooking time.

For gammon:

- 3 tablespoons of apricot jam, 4 ready-to-eat apricots finely chopped, ¼ teaspoon of ground cloves and 2 tablespoons of brandy or pineapple juice.

- 3 tablespoons of Chinese plum sauce, 2 cloves of crushed garlic, a ¼ teaspoon of chilli powder and 2 tablespoons of orange juice.

- Melt 2 tablespoons of fine-cut marmalade with 2 tablespoons of whisky. Brush over the gammon and then sprinkle over a little brown sugar.

For pork:

- 3 tablespoons of apple purée, ½ teaspoon of ground allspice and 2 tablespoons of rum or cranberry juice.

- 2 tablespoons of marmalade, 2 tablespoons of mandarin orange segments (skinned) and 2 tablespoons of Cointreau or apple juice.

For beef:

- 3 tablespoons of cranberry sauce, ½ teaspoon of ground cinnamon and 3 tablespoons of cassis or blackcurrant juice.

- 2 tablespoons of blackcurrant jam, ½ glass of red wine and a teaspoon of creamed horseradish.

Warm potato salad

Serves 6

700g/1½lb baby new potatoes, boiled in their skins
2tbsp fresh mint
3tbsp olive oil
Freshly ground black pepper

Boil the potatoes and drain. Immediately add the fresh mint and olive oil and swirl the pan to coat the potatoes with the dressing. Season with freshly ground black pepper. Transfer to a serving dish and serve immediately.

Christmas coleslaw

Serves 8 to 10

½ small red cabbage, quartered, stalks removed, and finely shredded

¼ crisp white cabbage, quartered, stalks removed, and finely shredded

400g/14oz carrots, peeled and grated

75g/3oz sultanas

50g/2oz dried cranberries

400g can chickpeas, drained and rinsed

A large handful of fresh coriander and flat-leaf parsley

For the dressing

6tbsp extra-virgin olive oil

2tbsp wine or sherry vinegar

Juice of a small orange

1tsp sugar

Freshly ground black pepper.

1. Prepare the red and white cabbage and the carrots and place in a large bowl. Mix well and add the sultanas, cranberries and chickpeas, then mix to combine.

2. Place the ingredients for the dressing in a screw-top jar then shake well to combine.

3. If you are ready to serve the coleslaw add the dressing, coriander and parsley to the bowl. Mix together and transfer to a glass serving dish so that the brilliant colours can be admired.

You can prepare the salad up to two days in advance and store in a sealed container in the fridge. Add the dressing and the coriander about an hour before serving.

(If you've got a shredding and grating attachment on your food processor make use of it – it's much quicker.)

Quick meals from leftovers

However carefully we shop we inevitably end up with food in the fridge and the larder after the holiday. Here are some simple ways to use it for quick meals and snacks.

Smoked salmon

Make a simple smoked salmon tagliatelli

- To serve four, fry a couple of sliced garlic cloves in a tablespoon of oil. Add 150ml leftover white wine and boil for 2 to 3 minutes. Add a small carton of double cream and 225g/8oz smoked salmon and simmer gently for 2 minutes. Stir in 4 portions of drained cooked tagliatelli and 225g/8oz washed baby spinach leaves and heat to piping hot. Place in four serving bowls topped with strips of smoked salmon. Serve with a green salad

Turkey

- For a simple lunch for two make a turkey sandwich with a difference. Lightly oil a large frying pan and place a flour tortilla in the bottom. Spread with cranberry sauce, mango chutney (or any other sweet chutney). Top with shredded turkey, thinly sliced red onion, and grated cheddar cheese.

  Place a second flour tortilla on the top, sandwich fashion. Brush the top of the tortilla with a little oil.

  Fry the tortilla sandwich on both sides until golden and crisp. Cut in half, transfer to plates and serve with a salad.

- Make a tasty soup with the turkey bones and leftover vegetables. Serve with warmed crusty bread.

Vegetables

- Cut any leftover vegetables into small pieces and sauté in a large nonstick frying pan to accompany cold meats. Or toss the sauté vegetables into a large Yorkshire pudding and pour gravy over.

Christmas pudding

- Add nuggets of Christmas pudding to stewed apples. Sprinkle over a crumble topping and bake for 35 to 40 minutes in a moderate oven (180°C/Gas 4) until the topping is golden.

Cheddar cheese

- Mix grated Cheddar with chopped pickled onion and drained crushed pineapple. Spread on toast, and pop under the grill until the cheese is melted and golden.

- Combine grated cheese with white breadcrumbs, and sprinkle over a dish of steamed broccoli and cauliflower. Pop under a hot grill or in the oven until the cheese has melted and the breadcrumbs are golden.

- Grate and freeze to add to soups and sauces when the holiday is over.

Camembert and Brie

- Make a toastie. Cut two thick slices of granary bread. Top one piece with a slice of gammon, add a few pieces of cheese and cover with the second slice of bread. Serve with a handful of grapes.

- Mix some cheese with a little wine, place in a ramekin and bake until gooey. Serve with crusty bread and a green leafy salad.

- Place a chunk of cheese on to a hot steak or pork chop and let it melt.

- Melt some cheese in a pan and pour over boiled new baby potatoes as soon as they have been drained.

- Lightly butter two thick slices of bread from a granary loaf or bloomer. Lay them on a board with the buttered sides down. Lay slices of Camembert or Brie on the unbuttered side of one slice of bread. Spread cranberry sauce on the other slice of bread. Sandwich together and fry for 2 minutes each side until the toast is golden and the cheese melted. Place on a plate, cut in half and serve with a small salad for a quick lunch.

Fruit

Christmas is over and your fruit bowl is still overflowing. Here are some delicious ways to use it.

- Bottle clementines in a liqueur syrup to serve with ice cream or cream.

- Squeeze oranges and drink the juice – it'll boost your vitamin C levels.

- Freeze pears in slices to make tarts, pies and upside-down puddings. Make some chutney or poach whole pears in leftover red wine.

- Top breakfast cereal with yogurt and chopped fruit.

- Bananas can be made into banana cakes and frozen. Add them to curries or to flapjacks and muffins. Or freeze in slices and use to make quick breakfast smoothies when you're in a hurry.

New Year

Deciding how to celebrate the New Year can be a dilemma. Some people could not bear to let the New Year arrive without a bit of a shindig, while others see it as the perfect chance to relax and unwind after the excitement and hard work of the Christmas festivities.

New Year's Eve parties at home have changed over the years. Large and lively extravaganzas have given way to smaller gatherings of friends and family who live near enough to be able to get a taxi home after the party, or can stay over.

If you decide to invite friends or family round for a New Year's Eve supper or dinner, why not ask them to bring along an item which reminds them of the old year to put into a time capsule? Seal all the items in a thick plastic bag with a note explaining what they are, and put them in a small tin box. At midnight creep out into the garden and bury it. (It might be a good idea to get the hole dug in advance in case the ground is frozen solid on New Year's Eve.)

Or there are plenty of other things you could do.

- Cook supper for your loved one, put on a new DVD and relax until it's time to listen to the chimes of Big Ben and crack open a bottle of bubbly.

- Get a group together and book dinner at a favourite restaurant.

- Get some friends round, order in a takeaway and watch some DVDs (remember to put your order in early).

- Have supper at home with friends then head off to an organised New Year's fireworks display.

- Spread the load. You make a main course and ask friends to bring the starter, dessert and perhaps the wine.

- Book a holiday and jet off to somewhere warm, or for some winter sports.

13

Christmas Games

Party Games

Party games – you love them or hate them! But to many people party games are an essential part of Christmas. So here are some you might like to add to your repertoire.

Who's in the box?

Each player writes the names of ten famous people, dead or alive, on slips of paper, folds them and puts them in a container. Players then split into teams. A member of the team that goes first pulls out a slip of paper and describes the name on the slip to his or her teammates (without saying the name, obviously), who have to guess the identity. They have one minute to guess as many as possible, after which the turn passes to the next team. Keep a note of how many your team gets right. When all the names have been pulled out, then you play the game again, only this time players can only use a single word to describe the famous person. Finally, when all the names have been pulled out for a second time, you can play the game one more time, only now players must use actions – no words or sounds – to describe the person. The winning team is the one which gets the most correct answers. With this game, it really pays to listen carefully in the first round!

Christmas lucky dip

This is a perfect way to get rid of all those hideous Christmas presents from last year! Collect together lots of small, inexpensive presents – the cheaper and sillier the better – wrap them all up and stick a raffle ticket/piece of paper with a number on it on each present. Make sure you have the same number of gifts for each guest, otherwise someone may get jealous! Put the corresponding tickets in a container. Then each person takes it in turns to pick out a ticket, and they get to keep the present with the number corresponding to their ticket.

Who am I?

Another celebrity guessing game. Each player takes a Post-it note or piece of paper and writes the name of a famous person on it. They then stick it to the forehead of the person sitting next to them, so that person can't see the name but the other players can. Each player then gets to ask the others a series of questions to try and work out who they are. The questions can only elicit a Yes or No answer from the other players e.g. Am I a man? Am I alive? The player's turn ends when the answer to their question is No, and the turn to ask questions passes to the next player. The winner is the player who guesses their identity correctly first, but you can keep going until there is only one person left.

'Are you there, Moriarty?'

This is a traditional parlour game, and although very silly it's hilarious to watch! Two players are blindfolded and given a rolled up newspaper – or something similar that's not likely to injure anyone – to use as a weapon. The players then lie on their backs head to head with about three feet of space between them. The starting player says 'Are you there, Moriarty?' The other player, when ready, says 'Yes'. At this point the players attempt to hit each other with their newspapers by swinging them over their heads. In order to avoid being hit, each player may roll to one side or the other. The game ends when one player successfully hits his or her opponent.

Only using your mouth . . .

Place an object on the floor – a good item to use is a cardboard cereal box or juice carton with the top cut off. Each player has to pick the object up off the floor using their teeth, but they can't put their hands, knees or any body part other than their feet on the floor. The idea is that you start off with something fairly big and easy to pick up and each round replace it with something smaller and closer to the ground. If you're using a cardboard box, each round you can cut a bit off so that the box gets smaller and smaller. If a player falls over or touches the floor, then they're out.

Under the table

Place eight items in separate resealable plastic bags. Give each of the guests a piece of paper and a pencil. The bags are passed in succession from person to person under the table. The idea is to feel each bag and decide what it contains before passing it on to the next person. When all eight items have been passed round each person writes down all of the items they managed to identify and remember. No one must write anything until all eight items have been passed round. The one who gets the most correct wins a small prize. The list of items you could put in the bags is endless – a small ball of wool, a knobbly stem of ginger, a date, a sponge . . .

You're never fully dressed without a smile

One player is selected to be 'it'. That person is the only one in the group who is allowed to smile. He or she can do anything they want to try and get someone else to smile, apart from touching them. If the person smiles, he or she becomes it. The person who never smiles is the winner.

The Minister's cat

A game that tests your word power and memory. The first player starts by saying: 'The Minister's cat is an angry cat,' then the next player repeats the sentence but replaces the adjective 'angry' with another adjective beginning with the letter A, for example, 'The Minister's cat is an arrogant cat.' Other players continue in turn, each using a different adjective beginning with the letter A. When a player cannot think of a word or repeats one that has already been used, they have to drop out, and everyone else moves on to B, C and so on through the alphabet, until only one player is left – the winner.

14

Out and About

The temptation at Christmas is to toast your toes in front of a roaring log fire or curl up and watch the television. But resist and make the effort to get out and about. If you hunt around you'll find there is a surprising amount going on. Get out and meet friends, visit the theatre or a panto, take in a concert, visit a special Christmas event in a nearby town or city. Or wrap up and get out into the fresh air – even if it's just to kick a ball in the park.

If you're looking for a day out in the weeks before Christmas search out a Christmas market, festival, craft fayre, food fair or farmers' market near you. And if you're a sucker for twinkling lights, Glühwein, marzipan and gingerbread you'll be in your element at one of the hundreds of Continental markets in towns and cities the length and breadth of the land. Some of the events last just a day or two but others run for several weeks. For information on Christmas markets in the UK go to www.christmasmarkets.com/list_markets. asp, or check in your local paper or at the library.

Almost every town now boasts a Christmas market but here are some of the Christmas festivals, craft and food fairs.

Festivals, craft and food fairs

Ballymoney Fine Food and Craft Fair

Birmingham Christmas Craft Market

Blenheim Palace Living Crafts for Christmas

Burghley House, Crafts for Christmas

Caerphilly Medieval Christmas Fayre

Cardiff Christmas Festival

Christmas Crafts at Broadlands, Hampshire

Cirencester Advent Festival and Market

Doncaster Christmas Fine Food and Gift Fayre

Durham City Christmas Festival

Frost Fair, Southwark

Grassington Dickensian Festival

Hestercombe Garden Christmas Fayre

Hodenby Festive Food Fayre

Kent Christmas Food Fayre, Bexley

Keswick Victorian Fayre

Leeds Castle Festive Food and Craft Fayre

Llandudno Celtic Winter Fayre

Ludlow Castle Food and Craft Fayre, Aldbridge

Made in York Christmas Crafts, York

Manchester Arts and Crafts Market

Michelham Priory Christmas Craft and Gift Fayre, Hailsham

Newcastle Christmas Craft Market

Physic Garden Christmas Fayre, Chelsea

Portsmouth Victorian Festival of Christmas

RHS Wisley Crafts for Christmas

Skipton Medieval Yuletide Festival

Stamford Arts and Crafts market

Ulverston Victorian Fayre

Wakefield Victorian Festival

York Children's Christmas Fayre

Other ideas to get you out and about at Christmas

- Take the children to see the brightest display of Christmas lights near you and treat them to supper at their favourite eatery.

- Step back in time. Visit a historic house or property and see how the wealthy spent their Christmases in years gone by. And discover what life was like for the servants below stairs. Many historic homes run fantastic programmes of special events in the weeks up to Christmas.

- If your town or city has an ice rink spend a couple of hours on the ice. It's great fun, and good exercise as well.

- Treat the children to a visit to Santa's grotto. There's sure to be one near you. If there isn't, see if the white-bearded gentleman in red is paying a whistle-stop visit to a local Christmas event.

- Look for an artificial ski slope to get in some practice if you're planning a winter sports holiday.

- Get together with friends or the family and book tickets to a panto or Christmas show.

- Make time to attend a Christmas carol concert.

- Be a 'tourist' in your own town. It's amazing how many of us seem to ignore the interesting places on our own doorstep. Go to your town's tourist information office and pick up some leaflets. You're sure to find a walk, a museum, gallery or historic building or garden you haven't visited – or even heard about.

- If there is a nature reserve near you see if the local wardens are arranging any guided walks over the Christmas and New Year period.

- Wrap up warm, visit a local beauty spot, climb a hill, walk along a river. You'll be amazed at how much there is to see.

- Meet up with friends for a walk and a pub lunch.

- Head for the sales – if it's before Christmas you might pick up some last-minute gifts and if it's after Christmas why not treat yourself? After all your hard work you deserve it.

- Have an afternoon at the movies. Either book tickets to the cinema or get in the children's favourite film and watch it on DVD. Give them paper cups filled with homemade or bought popcorn.

- Seek out a long-forgotten friend and arrange to meet for a New Year drink.

- If you are still stuck for things to do and looking for inspiration get online. Type 'things to do Christmas UK' – you'll find an avalanche of ideas so be prepared for a long read. Or log on to the tourist board site for your area and check out Christmas events.

15

Resources and Other Useful Information

Dealing with a Christmas crisis

The turkey won't fit in the oven

Try removing the legs and putting them in a separate roasting tray. If this doesn't work cut the turkey in half using a sharp serrated knife. Put each of the halves into a roasting tray (cut sides down) and cook side by side if there is room, or one at a time. Remember to recalculate the cooking time.

The turkey is overcooked

Slice as much turkey as you need and arrange on a large serving platter. Pour over some gravy and place in a low oven (150C/Gas 2) for 10 minutes. The meat will absorb some of the gravy and become beautifully moist.

The roast potatoes have burned

If they aren't too badly burned cut off the burned pieces. If they are beyond saving, whip out some frozen roasties (make sure you have some in the freezer for emergencies). Defrost them in the microwave and put them into a hot oven until they are crisp and golden. It should only take about 20 minutes. (Give everyone another drink and they won't notice that lunch is running a little late.)

The Brussels sprouts are overcooked

Crush them lightly and sprinkle over some melted butter and chopped toasted hazelnuts. Everyone will think that is how you intended to serve them.

The gravy is too thin

Place a knob of butter in a small bowl. Add an equal quantity of plain flour, then mix together to make a stiff paste. Break off a small piece of paste and stir it into the gravy. Bring to the boil. Continue adding more small pieces of the paste until you have the required consistency (or get out the trusty gravy granules from the store cupboard!).

No room in the fridge

Perishable goods such as meat, poultry, fish, dairy products, creamy puddings and ready-prepared meals must go in the fridge.

But you can move the drinks, vegetables and fruit into cardboard boxes and keep them in a cool place like the garage, a shed, or even the boot of the car.

What to do if you receive an unexpected gift

Have a couple of unisex gifts for adults and children ready-wrapped for just such an occasion. Wine, chocolates, luxury biscuits, picture frames and book and iTune tokens are great standbys. If they aren't needed you can always make use of them or put them away for birthdays.

Stains and spills

The secret of stain removal is SPEED. Have a basic stain-removing kit on standby – many of the items will already be in your kitchen:

- A bottle of soda water – to dilute the stains
- Kitchen towel or pieces of old towel cut into large pieces – to soak up wet spills before you remove the stain
- Lemon
- Salt
- Soap flakes (for delicate items)
- Biological detergent
- Laundry borax
- Talcum powder

Candle wax

If the fabric is washable and the stained item is small, place it into a plastic bag, seal the top and pop into the freezer to harden the wax. Then scrape off the wax with a blunt knife. If any wax remains place a thick pad of absorbent paper or a brown paper bag under the stain and another pad on top, and press with a warm iron. Finally wash the garment. If the garment is too large to put in the freezer try to remove the stain using the paper and iron method.

If the wax is on upholstery or a non-washable item, try to set the wax using ice cubes and gently scrape off as much as you can. Use the iron and paper method to remove any remaining wax.

If wax is spilled on carpet scrape up as much as you can then harden any left by placing a bag of ice over the stain. Pick the hardened wax from the carpet fibres. If any wax remains use the paper and iron method until the paper has absorbed the wax.

> **Stain removal tip**
>
> **Try to work on the wrong side of the fabric. Place a pad of towel under the stain and work from the outside to the centre of the mark to prevent it from spreading.**

Fats

If the item is washable remove any visible grease, taking care not to spread the mark. Dab with eucalyptus oil then wash as usual.

Delicate and non-washable fabrics can be dabbed with a little eucalyptus oil and then washed at a low temperature. If fat is spilled on upholstered furniture, sprinkle talcum powder over the mark. Leave for thirty minutes then brush off the powder. Repeat until the stain has been removed.

For fat stains on carpet cover the spot with talcum powder. Leave for a few hours and then vacuum. If traces of the stain remain, sprinkle a few drops of eucalyptus oil on to a clean cloth and dab the stain.

Red wine

If the garment is washable lay it on a flat surface and pour salt on to the stain to stop it spreading, then soak in cold water. If the garment is still stained soak in a borax solution and then wash as usual.

If the fabric cannot be washed sponge with a dry sponge dipped in soda water and blot with a folded towel to remove as much water as possible. Repeat until the stain is removed. If red wine is spilled on carpet blot the area and pour on soda water or white wine. Blot immediately with a pad of towel to remove as much liquid as possible. Repeat until the stain is removed. Finally, clean with carpet shampoo. Some carpets may need special treatment. White vinegar can be used on white wine stains.

Tip
Warning – if you are unsure about the kind of fabric, or if it is valuable, always seek advice from the experts before attempting to remove stains.

Home security

Thieves are always on the lookout for easy pickings at Christmas and when you're busy it's easy to let your usual good habits slip.

So remember to:

- Always lock your windows, doors and garage every time you leave the house – even if it's just to pop next door to borrow a packet of sugar!

- Make sure wrapped presents cannot be seen from windows.

- Keep your handbag, wallet and keys away from the front door. Opportunistic thieves can open a door and lift valuables from the hall in seconds.

- Never leave your keys in a 'safe' place like under a mat or a flowerpot. Thieves know all of these places.

- Keep your garden shed and garage locked – tools and ladders stored in them could be used to get into your house. If your ladder won't fit into the garage, padlock it to something that cannot be moved.

- Never leave a note on your door saying you are out, or telling the postman to deliver parcels to a neighbour.

- Be vigilant about callers. Never let anyone into your house if they are unable to show you satisfactory identification. If you are not sure, send them away and call the company they say they represent to arrange another visit.

Domestic emergencies

Unblocking a sink

If water will not drain away, bale it out of the sink into a bucket. Pile two cups of washing-soda crystals over the drain hole and slowly pour a kettle of boiling water over the crystals. If this does not clear the blockage repeat the process.

If the blockage still does not move you will need to use a sink plunger. It's a good idea to have an inexpensive vacuum plunger sitting in the garage for these emergencies.

Place the plunger directly over the drain hole. Push down very firmly then pull up rapidly, keeping the plunger over the hole all the time. Repeat several times until the blockage clears. Put some soda crystals over the drain hole and pour over boiling water to flush out the pipe.

If the blockage is in the U-bend under the sink you may need to unscrew it. Place a bucket or bowl under the pipe to catch any water before you unscrew it. Wash out the U-bend and check there is no blockage either side of the pipe. If it is clear replace the U-bend.

If this does not work you will need to call a plumber, as the blockage will be somewhere else in your pipes. Clearing blockages to pipes outside generally requires the use of drain rods, so this is probably another job you will want to pass on to the plumber.

Frozen pipes

Frozen pipes should be thawed as soon as possible to prevent them cracking.

Turn the water off at the mains and turn on any taps fed from the frozen pipe. Feel along the pipe to find the point that is frozen. If the pipe is metal use a hairdryer on a warm setting and hold it close to the pipe. When thawing plastic pipes take care not to let the pipe become very hot or it may melt.

Prevent pipes from freezing by ensuring that vulnerable pipes are lagged.

Do you know where to turn your water, electricity and gas supplies off at the mains?

If you don't, get someone to show you NOW. It is very important that you should know where they are and how they work.

Festive foliage

When you go to the garden centre for your summer plants, pick up a few evergreen shrubs that have attractive leaves and winter berries that you can harvest for your Christmas decorations.

- **Aucuba japonica** – a laurel-like shrub that can grow to over two metres (about seven feet).

- **Choisya** (Mexican orange blossom) – attractive green foliage. Look out for *Choisya terrnata*.

- **Cotoneaster** – these have berries in a variety of colours: *C. cornubia* (red berries), *C. rothschildianus* (yellow berries) and *C. franchetii* (deep orange berries).

- **Danae** – dark shiny green leaves and bright orange-red berries in winter.

- **Eucalyptus** (gum tree) – this can be pruned in the spring to maintain it as a shrub with the distinctive oval blue-green juvenile foliage often used in arrangements, or allowed to grow into a tree, which then has long dainty leaves.

- **Hebe** – there are a wide variety, many of which provide attractive foliage to use in arrangements.

- **Ilex** (Holly) – holly is slow-growing. Buy a small plant and wait for it to grow, as holly doesn't enjoy being transplanted.

- **Ivy** – there are many varieties of ivy. If you want to keep it under control grow it in a container with a fan support, or against a fence. *Laurus* (Bay laurel) – female plants have black berries in autumn. The variety *L. nobilis* can stand drastic pruning.

- **Pyracantha** (Firethorn) – the small waxy leaves and clusters of tiny berries are perfect in Christmas arrangements. Look out for *Pyracantha* orange glow (bright orange red berries), *P. watererii* (bright red berries) and *P. rogersiani* 'Flava' (yellow berries).

- **Skimmia** – a neat and compact shrub which is good in containers. The dark oval leaves and large red berries are excellent in Christmas arrangements. Look for a self-fertile variety such as *S. fortunei*.

A Family Christmas Scrapbook

Create a Family Christmas scrapbook to record the highlights of your celebrations year by year. Filled with photographs and notes of the special memories, it will become a unique family heirloom, mirroring the changes in your family's tastes, interests and lifestyle. It's so much more than a diary.

Why not start your own scrapbook this year?

Look out for an attractive hard-backed notebook filled with blank pages to use. (There's a wide selection at stationers or on the web: try www.justamemory.co.uk)

Here are some ideas of what you could include each year:

- Photos of your beautifully decorated tree, the welcoming wreath on your door, an arrangement or decoration you were particularly proud of, the children opening their presents, the family Christmas lunch, the parties, your guests, a post-Christmas outing

- Your Christmas dinner menu and other special meals

- Notes about who visited you and visits you made to family and friends

- Ask the children to write about 'the best bits' of their Christmas or to draw a picture to be stuck into the book

Tips

- Work out what you plan to write on a piece of rough paper first so you don't have to reach for the correcting fluid

- Find yourself a pen you enjoy using

- Plan your pages in advance so that you leave enough room for your photos

- Use spray adhesive to stick photos into your book

- Trim your photos and cut some of them into different shapes to add interest

Resources

Food

Waitrose (0800 188884)
www.waitrose.co.uk

Marks & Spencer (0845 302 1234)
www.marksandspencer.com

Tesco (0800 505555)
www.tesco.com

Sainsbury's (0800 636262)
www.sainsburys.co.uk

Asda (0500 10055)
www.asda.co.uk

Morrisons (0845 611 61111)
www.morrisons.co.uk

Specialist foods

Hotel Chocolat
www.hotelchocolat.co.uk

La Fromagerie (0207 359 7440)
www.lafromagerie.co.uk

Valvonna & Crolla (0131 556 6066
www.valvonacrolla-online.co.uk

The Simply Delicious Fruit Cake Co (01584 823 679)
www.simplydeliciouscakes.co.uk

Fortnum & Mason (020 7734 8040)
www.fortnumandmason.com

Donald Russell (01467 629666)
www.donaldrussell.com

Ishmael's Mother (01372 813053)
www.ishmaelsmother.com

Cook (01732 770315)
www.cookfood.net

Drinks

The Drink Shop
www.thedrinkshop.com

Virgin Wines
www.virginwines.com

Drinks Direct
www.drinksdirect.co.uk

Chateau Online (0800 169 2736)
www.chateauonline.co.uk

Majestic Wine (01923 298200)
www.majestic.co.uk

Decorations, gifts and handicraft supplies

Paperchase (0207 7467 6200)
www.paperchase.co.uk

The Party Store (0845 055 1692)
www.partystore.co.uk

W.H. Smith (0870 444 6444)
www.whsmith.co.uk

The Pier (0845 609 1234)
www.pier.co.uk

The White Company (0870 900 9555)
www.thewhitecompany.com

John Lewis (0845 604 9049)
www.johnlewis.com

Celebration Cakes, Cranleigh (01483 277 199)

House of Fraser (0845 602 1073)
www.houseoffraser.co.uk

Lakeland Limited (015394 88100)
www.lakelandlimited.co.uk

Debenhams (0207 7408 4444)
www.debenhams.com

Boots (0845 070 8090)
www.boots.com

Manns of Cranleigh (01483 273 777)
www.mannsofcranleigh.co.uk

Champneys
www.champneysgift.com

Burntwood Kennels, Godalming (01483 200217)

Classic Crackers, Bicknoller (01984 656 464)
www.classic-crackers.co.uk

Inspiring Ideas
www.inspiring-ideas.co.uk

Gadsby Basketware (01278 437 123)
www.gadsby.co.uk

One Forty (01483 272 627)
www.oneforty.co.uk

The Haberdashery, Ramsgate, Kent
(01843 591617)

Pedlars (01330 850400)
www.pedlars.co.uk

Cox & Cox (0870 442 4787)
www.coxandcox.co.uk

Hobby Craft (0800 027 2387)
www.hobbycraft.co.uk

Aspinal of London (0845 052 6900)
www.aspinaloflondon.co.uk

Personalised stamps

Rubber Stampz
www.rubberstampz.co.uk

Stamp Factory
www.stampfactory.co.uk

Blade Rubber Stamps (0207 7831 4123)
www.bladerubberstamps.co.uk

Cake decoring

Squires Kitchen (0845 225 5671)
www.squires-shop.com

For information

Books for Cooks (0207 221 1992)
www.booksforcooks.com

British Turkey Information Service
(0800 783 9994)
www.britishturkey.co.uk

Seafish (0131 558 3331)
www.seafish.co.uk

The Soil Association (0117 929 0661)
www.soilassociation.org.uk

Christmas Checklist

Take Christmas in your stride with this handy checklist. These are just some ideas to get started, but if you have any other inspired ideas when reading this book then make a note of them here.

January

Keep a few Christmas cards so you can make gift tags with the children. Recycle the rest

Pick up wrapping paper, cards, string, ribbon and trimmings – and even decorations – in the sales at knock-down prices

Keep your eyes open for Christmas presents in the New Year sales

October

If you're making your own cards, get a design and start making them

If you're planning to use caterers, make your bookings as early as you can

Take a walk in the country and look for cones and seed heads to use in arrangements

Book tickets to pantomimes, the theatre and concerts

Make a note of any local Christmas events you plan to attend – don't forget school events

November

Buy or make your advent calendar

Order your Christmas turkey, goose and other meat

Dry orange slices for arrangements

Start your present buying in earnest, if you haven't already

Take any clothes that need cleaning to the cleaners

December

Make or buy any frozen desserts
you will need

Order flowers or plants for
gifts and arrange to have them
delivered nearer Christmas

Check your herbs and spices to see you
have everything you need. Discard
any that are past their use by date

Make festive biscuits and cakes for gifts

Check you've got in all the drinks you'll
need, including a variety of soft drinks

Christmas Eve

Arrange hand made chocolates in attractive
dishes to serve after dinner.

Help the children to make a snack for
Santa and his reindeers

Notes

Decoration templates

Here are some templates you can use to help you make the heart and flower decorations on page 40.

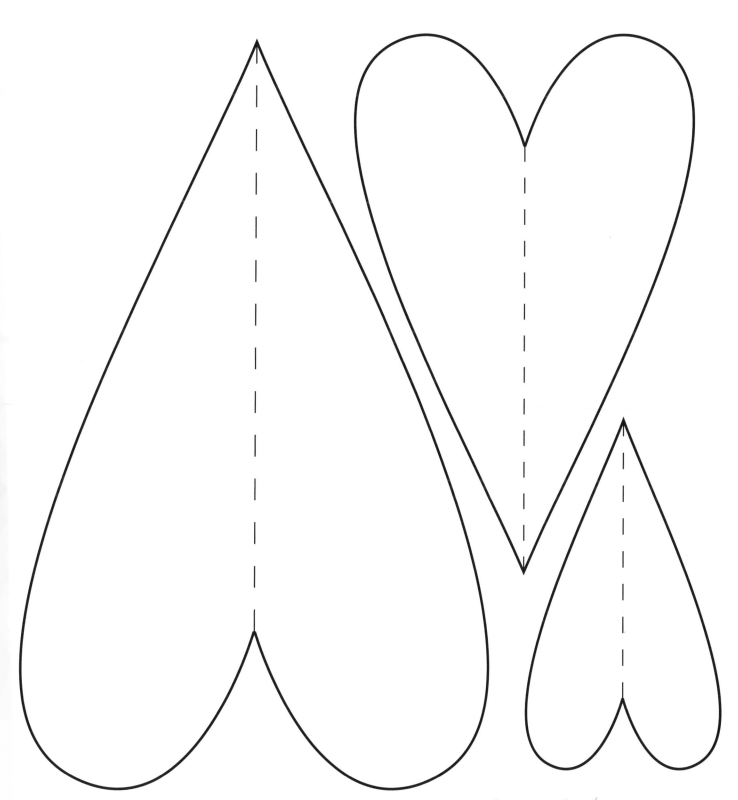

Acknowledgements

To the wonderful team who helped me put this delicious book together. They include: Alex Schneiderman, a gifted photographer, and his assistant Orlando Gili who ate all the roast potatoes on page 145, Carla Milner for her artistic flair and announcing on the shoot she was pregnant (this is her first Christmas as a mum), Amanda Armstrong and Lisa Cantrill, the two angels who keep me sane, Lauren Beale for keeping the beads of sweat off my forehead, Elaine Graham at One Forty Cranleigh High Street, for helping me to make my house in March look like December, Celebration Cakes of Cranleigh and Burnt Wood Kennels, Heather and Carina Norris, Michael Joyce, and the brilliant team at Virgin Books.

Charlie and Gabriel Lindsay for their smiling faces on page 52, my goddaughter Amber Skye (don't mess with me) Westgate on page 183, my nephews Jack and Freddy Webster who enthusiastically took part in Christmas card making and cooking (who said child labour has been abolished in this country?), Simon our blow up tacky snowman who never melts and comes out every Christmas on page 171, Digger and Buddie our two golden retrievers on page 56 whose will power (i.e. not eating the bones in front of them) was stretched to the limit by Alex.

Finally Grant, Lily, Amelia and Claudia for giving me a reason to clean, tidy and organise 'stuff'.

Index

Index (Cont.)